MAGNETIC MESSAGE MOVES

By: T.N Daman

Disclaimer

I

Table of Contents

Introduction

This book isn't a collection of jokes or my personal tales. It's about mastering the skill of storytelling first, then learning how to turn those stories into sales. I mean honing and expressing your unique personal or brand message as a powerful tool for preaching, marketing, selling, coaching, speaking, creating content, or growing any community of believers. That's why all the stories in this book are true; some examples are taken straight from the Holy Bible to ensure the truth and light are woven into this amazing Magnetic Message Mastering Tool Blueprint.

Throughout my career, I've had the privilege of sharing countless stories. While I enjoy writing, I'm even more fascinated by the power of storytelling. Stories can transport us to different worlds, stir emotions, and inspire action. They have a unique ability to connect us like nothing else can. But storytelling isn't just about entertaining or inspiring; it's also about selling.

In this book, I want to share with you a unique secret for marketing, preaching, speaking, and selling through narrative. Whether you're a marketer, a salesperson, an entrepreneur, or anyone else trying to convince, influence, and sell, understanding storytelling can be your key. I'll show you how to craft gripping, engaging stories that turn strangers into believers and customers into buyers.

1

Human Traditions

Throughout history, human life has been shaped by tradition. Passed down through generations, these customs are our cultural heritage, connecting us to our past and linking us with those who came before us. Traditions are not just habits; they are rich sources of wisdom and identity.

In today's fast-moving world, dominated by technology and short attention spans, the importance of tradition is often forgotten. Yet, despite the noise of modern life, storytelling remains a timeless tradition. It crosses boundaries and speaks to our very core.

From ancient cave paintings to today's digital media, stories have always been with us, guiding and reflecting us. They illuminate our past, highlighting the victories and struggles of our ancestors. Stories create a shared memory that unites us as humans.

I remember my childhood evenings by the fire, captivated by my grandmother's tales. Her stories were not just for fun; they were glimpses into our culture, opening doors to real and imagined worlds. Through her words, I learned about heroes and heroines, love and loss, and the eternal battle between good and evil.

One story that sticks with me is about Ntare Rushatsi Cambarantama, the legendary founder of the Burundian monarchy. Through my grandmother's vivid stories, I traveled through history, witnessing the rise and fall of dynasties, the clash of empires, and the enduring human spirit.

Storytelling isn't just a thing of the past; it's a vibrant art that shapes our present and future. In today's connected world, where information spreads quickly, stories are powerful. They help us understand our complex world, guiding us with wisdom.

My journey with storytelling deepened when I explored the Bible, a sacred book filled with 66 stories of divine wisdom. These stories of creation, redemption, love, and sacrifice touched my soul, offering comfort in dark times and guidance in uncertainty.

As an ethnographic research assistant, I had the chance to dive into diverse human cultures. From the busy markets of Marrakech to the remote villages of Papua New Guinea, I encountered vibrant traditions. These experiences taught me the profound impact of storytelling on the human mind.

Everywhere on Earth, from the Arctic tundra to the Amazon jungle, stories are found—tales of survival, love, hope, and despair. They are the essence of our existence, weaving us into a shared human tapestry.

One of the most memorable moments of my travels was sitting with an elder in a small village in Papua New Guinea. He spoke of his ancestors with such reverence and depth, sharing tales that had been passed down for centuries. His stories were filled with the spirit of his people, their struggles, and their triumphs. It was in these moments that I realized how storytelling keeps cultures alive and vibrant.

In this chapter, "Human Traditions," I invite you to explore storytelling. We will learn how to craft narratives that resonate with people everywhere. We will uncover the techniques and tools perfected over millennia, unlocking the secrets of compelling storytelling and its transformative power.

Storytelling is not just an art; it's a skill that can be learned and honed. It involves understanding your audience, knowing the right moments to add suspense or emotion, and finding the right words to convey your message. We will explore different storytelling techniques, such as the use of metaphors, symbolism, and pacing.

For instance, consider the way a simple metaphor can transform a story. When my grandmother described the bravery of a hero, she often compared their courage to that of a lion, fierce and unyielding. This simple comparison painted a vivid picture in my young mind, making the hero's bravery feel almost tangible.

Moreover, the structure of a story is crucial. A well-told story has a beginning that captures attention, a middle that builds tension, and an end that provides resolution. This structure, often referred to as the "story arc," is a timeless blueprint that ensures the audience remains engaged from start to finish.

In the end, stories help us discover our true humanity, the timeless quality that connects us all. So, let's embark on this journey together, unraveling the mysteries of the human soul and celebrating the rich tapestry of human tradition.

Through this journey, you will not only learn how to tell better stories but also how to listen to them with a deeper appreciation. Listening is as much a part of storytelling as speaking. By truly hearing the stories of others, we open ourselves to new perspectives and understandings.

So, as we dive into the world of human traditions and storytelling, remember that each story you hear or tell is a thread in the larger tapestry of human experience. Let's celebrate these threads and the rich, diverse fabric they create. Let's honor the traditions that have shaped us and continue to shape the generations to come. Together, we will keep the art of storytelling alive, vibrant, and ever-evolving.

2

Story Characters

Stories are like magic carpets that sweep us away to far-off lands, introduce us to fascinating characters, and immerse us in captivating adventures. They're the heartbeats of human experience, pulsating with emotion, insight, and imagination. But what's the secret sauce that makes a story truly magnetic? What draws us in and keeps us spellbound?

In this chapter, we're going to dive deep into the enchanting world of storytelling. We'll unravel the mystery behind why stories have such a powerful grip on our hearts and minds, and we'll uncover the essential elements that make a story come alive.

So, grab your imagination by the hand and let's embark on this exhilarating journey together!

Characters: The Heroes and Villains of Our Tales:

First up, let's talk about characters—the beating heart of any story. Think of your favorite stories. What is it about the characters that resonates with you? Maybe it's Harry Potter's unwavering bravery, Katniss Everdeen's fierce determination, or Sherlock Holmes' razorsharp intellect. Characters are the soul of a story, the ones we root for, love, hate, and sometimes even love to hate.

Creating compelling characters is like sculpting a masterpiece out of clay. You start with a rough idea—an outline of who they are, what they want, and what stands in their way. Then, you layer on details, quirks, and contradictions until they leap off the page and into the reader's heart.

But what makes a character truly magnetic? It's not just about giving them a cool name or a tragic backstory (though those certainly help). It's about making them feel real, flawed, and oh-so-human. We want characters who struggle, grow, and change over the course of the story. Characters who are as messy and complicated as we are.

Take Frodo Baggins, for example. At first glance, he might seem like an unlikely hero—a small, unassuming hobbit thrust into a world of magic and danger. But it's precisely because of his flaws and vulnerabilities that we can't help but root for him. We see ourselves in Frodo—the doubts, fears, and moments of courage that define his journey resonate with our own.

And let's not forget about the villains—the dark shadows lurking in the corners of our imagination. A great villain is more than just a mustache-twirling caricature. They're complex, driven by motives that are as twisted as they are compelling. Think of Hannibal Lecter, Darth Vader, or the Wicked Witch of the West. These villains are so memorable because they're more than just obstacles for the hero to overcome— they're reflections of our darkest desires and fears.

Crafting Your Cast of Characters:

So, how do you go about creating characters that leap off the page and into your reader's heart? It all starts with asking the right questions. Who is your character? What do they want more than anything in the world? What's standing in their way? What are their hopes, dreams, and fears?

Once you've got a handle on the basics, it's time to dig deeper. Give your characters quirks, flaws, and contradictions that make them feel human. Maybe your protagonist has a fear of spiders or a tendency to burst into song at the most inappropriate moments. Maybe your villain is a hopeless romantic or secretly harbors a fear of failure.

And don't forget about character arcs—the journey of growth and transformation that your characters embark on over the course of the story. Whether it's Frodo's gradual descent into darkness or Darth Vader's redemption arc, character arcs add depth and nuance to your story, keeping readers invested from beginning to end.

Plot, Setting, and Theme: The Building Blocks of Storytelling:

Of course, characters are just one piece of the storytelling puzzle. To truly craft a magnetic story, you'll need to master the art of plot, setting, and theme.

Plot is the engine that drives your story forward, the series of events that keep readers on the edge of their seats. It's the quest to destroy the One Ring, the battle for survival in a dystopian arena, the epic showdown between good and evil. A great plot keeps readers guessing, throwing unexpected twists and turns their way until the very last page.

But a compelling plot is nothing without a rich and detailed setting to bring it to life. Whether it's the bustling streets of Victorian London, the sprawling galaxies of a distant future, or the eerie quiet of a haunted house, setting adds texture, atmosphere, and mood to your story. It's the backdrop against which your characters' lives unfold, the stage on which the drama of your story plays out.

And let's not forget about theme—the deeper meaning and emotional resonance that gives your story its heart and soul. Whether it's the power of love, the nature of good and evil, or the importance of friendship, theme is the thread that ties your story together, weaving its way through every scene and character arc.

Bringing Your Story to Life:

Now that you've crafted your characters, plotted your story, and built your world, it's time to bring it all together and tell your story to the world. Whether you're writing a novel, a screenplay, or a comic book, storytelling is an art form that requires skill, passion, and perseverance.

But storytelling isn't just about putting words on a page—it's about connecting with your audience on a deep and emotional level. It's about making them laugh, cry, and gasp in surprise. It's about transporting them to a world of wonder and excitement, where anything is possible.

So, don't be afraid to experiment with different storytelling techniques—from vivid descriptions and snappy dialogue to heartpounding action sequences and quiet moments of introspection. Find your voice, trust your instincts, and above all, have fun!

And there you have it—the essential elements of crafting a magnetic story. Characters that leap off the page, a plot that keeps readers guessing, a setting that feels alive, and a theme that resonates with readers on a deep and emotional level. So, what are you waiting for? Grab your pen, your keyboard, or your trusty quill, and start telling your story to the world. After all, the world is waiting to be swept away by your imagination.

Supporting Character:

Supporting characters are often the unsung heroes of a story, providing crucial assistance, guidance, and encouragement to the protagonist. Their presence enriches the narrative, adding depth and complexity to the protagonist's journey.

In the Bible, we encounter numerous supporting characters whose roles are instrumental in advancing the overarching story of faith, redemption, and divine providence. One such character is Barnabas, whose name means "son of encouragement." Barnabas plays a pivotal role in the early Christian community, particularly in his relationship with the apostle Paul.

Barnabas first appears in the book of Acts, where he sells a field and donates the proceeds to support the fledgling Christian community in Jerusalem (Acts 4:36-37). His generous act sets the stage for his subsequent involvement in the spread of Christianity.

However, Barnabas's most significant contribution lies in his relationship with Paul. When Paul, formerly known as Saul, seeks to join the disciples in Jerusalem, they are wary of him due to his past persecution of Christians. It is Barnabas who vouches for Paul, affirming his conversion and facilitating his acceptance into the Christian community (Acts 9:26-27).

Barnabas continues to mentor and support Paul as they embark on missionary journeys together, preaching the gospel and establishing churches in various regions. Despite facing opposition and adversity, Barnabas remains steadfast in his commitment to Paul and their shared mission (Acts 13-14).

Another notable supporting character is Ruth, whose story unfolds in the Old Testament book bearing her name. Ruth, a Moabite widow, accompanies her mother-in-law Naomi back to Bethlehem after the death of their husbands. Despite the cultural and social challenges she faces as a foreigner, Ruth demonstrates unwavering loyalty and devotion to Naomi, declaring, "Where you go, I will go; where you stay, I will stay. Your people will be my people and your God my God" (Ruth

1:16).

Ruth's selfless commitment to Naomi leads her to glean in the fields of Boaz, a relative of Naomi's deceased husband. Boaz recognizes Ruth's character and integrity, and their eventual marriage not only secures Ruth's future but also ensures the continuation of Naomi's lineage. Through Ruth's faithfulness and Boaz's kindness, God orchestrates a beautiful story of redemption and restoration.

In our own lives, we can emulate the examples of Barnabas and Ruth by being supportive and encouraging to those around us. Whether it's offering a listening ear, providing practical assistance, or simply being present in times of need, we can make a meaningful difference in the lives of others.

Love Interest:

Love interests add an element of romance and emotional depth to a story, often serving as catalysts for character development and plot progression. In the Bible, love stories abound, showcasing the transformative power of love and its significance in the lives of God's people.

One of the most iconic love stories in the Bible is that of Ruth and Boaz, whose union exemplifies God's providential care and redemptive love. Ruth, a Moabite widow, finds herself in a foreign land after the death of her husband, where she meets Boaz, a wealthy landowner and relative of her deceased husband's family.

Despite their differences in social status and background, Ruth and Boaz form a deep connection based on mutual respect, kindness, and loyalty. Boaz's admiration for Ruth's virtuous character prompts him to extend special privileges to her, ensuring her safety and provision as she gleans in his fields.

As their relationship blossoms, Boaz becomes Ruth's kinsmanredeemer, fulfilling the role of a guardian and protector for her and Naomi. Their eventual marriage not only brings joy and fulfillment to Ruth and Boaz but also serves as a symbol of God's faithfulness in preserving the lineage of His chosen people.

Another compelling love story in the Bible is that of Esther and King Xerxes. Esther, a Jewish orphan raised by her cousin Mordecai, finds herself thrust into the royal court of Persia after winning the favor of King Xerxes in a beauty contest. Despite the political intrigue and danger surrounding her,

Esther's courage and wisdom capture the heart of the king, leading to her eventual elevation as queen.

Throughout her reign, Esther remains true to her identity and heritage, risking her life to intercede on behalf of her people when they face imminent destruction at the hands of the wicked Haman. King Xerxes's love for Esther prompts him to heed her pleas for mercy, resulting in the salvation of the Jewish people and the downfall of their enemies.

These biblical love stories serve as powerful reminders of the transformative nature of love and its ability to overcome adversity, bridge divides, and bring about redemption. In our own lives, we can draw inspiration from these stories as we navigate the complexities of love and relationships, seeking to embody the selfless love and sacrificial commitment exemplified by Ruth, Boaz, Esther, and King Xerxes.

Sidekick:

Sidekicks are often the unsung heroes of a story, providing comic relief, moral support, and practical assistance to the protagonist. While they may not always be the focal point of the narrative, their presence enriches the story and enhances the protagonist's journey.

In the Bible, we encounter several noteworthy sidekick characters who play instrumental roles in supporting and accompanying the main characters on their respective journeys of faith and destiny. One such character is Aaron, the older brother of Moses and his trusted companion in the mission to deliver the Israelites from bondage in Egypt.

Aaron serves as Moses's spokesperson and intermediary before Pharaoh, conveying God's messages and performing miraculous signs and wonders alongside his brother. Despite his occasional lapses in judgment, such as his role in the golden calf incident, Aaron remains a loyal and faithful ally to Moses, providing vital support and encouragement throughout their shared ordeal.

Another prominent sidekick character in the Bible is Barnabas, a companion of the apostle Paul during his missionary journeys and ministry endeavors. Barnabas, whose name means "son of encouragement," lives up to his moniker by nurturing and affirming Paul's calling as an apostle, even when others doubt or oppose him.

Barnabas's unwavering support and friendship bolster Paul's confidence and effectiveness in proclaiming the gospel, resulting in the establishment of numerous churches and the spread of Christianity throughout the Roman Empire. Despite their eventual parting ways due to a disagreement over John Mark's involvement in their mission, Barnabas's impact on Paul's life and ministry is undeniable, cementing his legacy as a beloved sidekick and faithful friend.

In our own lives, we can strive to emulate the examples of Aaron and Barnabas by offering steadfast support, encouragement, and companionship to those around us. Whether it's standing by a friend in times of adversity, lending a listening ear to someone in need, or simply being present as a source of comfort and solidarity, we can make a meaningful difference in the lives of others as faithful sidekicks and allies in the journey of faith.

Dynamic Character:

Dynamic characters undergo significant changes and growth throughout the course of a story, evolving in response to their experiences, challenges, and interactions with other characters. These characters often serve as vehicles for exploring themes of transformation, redemption, and personal development.

In the Bible, we encounter numerous dynamic characters whose journeys of faith and self-discovery serve as powerful examples of God's transformative work in the lives of His people. One such character is Joseph, whose story is chronicled in the book of Genesis.

Joseph begins his journey as the favored son of Jacob, but his brothers' jealousy and betrayal lead to his sale into slavery in Egypt. Despite facing adversity and hardship, Joseph remains faithful to God and demonstrates exemplary character, eventually rising to prominence as the second-in-command to Pharaoh.

Through a series of trials and tests, including false accusations and imprisonment, Joseph learns important lessons about forgiveness, humility, and the sovereignty of God. His reconciliation with his brothers and their eventual reunion serve as a testament to God's faithfulness and the power of forgiveness to heal broken relationships.

Another dynamic character in the Bible is David, whose rise from humble shepherd to renowned king of Israel is marked by triumphs and tribulations. David's faith journey is characterized by moments of courage, doubt, and repentance, as he grapples with the complexities of kingship and the consequences of his own actions.

Despite his flaws and failures, David's unwavering devotion to God and his willingness to acknowledge his mistakes set him apart as a man after God's own heart. Through his psalms and prayers, David pours out his soul to God, seeking forgiveness, guidance, and restoration.

Both Joseph and David exemplify the transformative power of faith and obedience, as they navigate the highs and lows of life with steadfast trust in God's providence and grace. Their stories remind us that growth and change are integral to the Christian journey, as we strive to become more like Christ in character and conduct.

In our own lives, we can embrace the role of dynamic characters by remaining open to God's leading and allowing Him to work in and through us for His glory. By surrendering our plans and desires to His will, we position ourselves to experience His transformative power and become instruments of His grace in the world.

In conclusion, the characters we encounter in stories, whether fictional or biblical, serve as mirrors reflecting our own human experiences, struggles, and triumphs. From protagonists and antagonists to mentors and sidekicks, each character contributes to the richness and depth of the narrative, inviting us to explore the complexities of the human condition and the enduring themes of love, redemption, and resilience.

As we engage with these characters and their stories, may we be inspired to embrace our own roles as protagonists in the grand adventure of life, trusting in God's providence and guidance every step of the way. Whether facing challenges or experiencing moments of triumph, may we find solace and strength in the knowledge that we are never alone, for God is with us, shaping our stories and weaving them into the tapestry of His divine plan.

With each character we encounter and each story we explore, may we glean wisdom, insight, and inspiration for our own journeys of faith and self-discovery. And may we, like the characters of old, leave a legacy of faith, hope, and love that endures for generations to come.

In this way, the characters of stories, both ancient and modern, continue to speak to us across the ages, reminding us of our shared humanity and our eternal quest for meaning, purpose, and connection. And in their voices, we hear echoes of the divine Author, who weaves together the threads of our lives into a masterpiece of grace and redemption, inviting us to join Him in the unfolding drama of His love.

By embracing the lessons and insights gleaned from the characters of stories, may we become more compassionate, empathetic, and resilient individuals, equipped to face whatever challenges and adventures lie ahead. And may the stories we tell and the characters we create reflect the beauty, truth, and goodness of the One who is the ultimate Author and Finisher of our faith.

3

Business Narrative

Imagine telling a story that not only captures attention but also builds a deep connection with your audience. That's the power of brand storytelling. It's about crafting a narrative that resonates with your customers, sets you apart from the competition, and creates an emotional bond with your audience.

So, why is brand storytelling so important?

In today's world, consumers are hit with thousands of marketing messages daily. Standing out can be tough. A well-crafted brand story cuts through the noise, making your brand memorable and meaningful. It's not just about selling a product; it's about creating an experience and fostering loyalty. Think about the brands you love – chances are, they tell a story that resonates with you on a deeper level.

Understanding Your Brand

To craft a compelling brand story, you first need to understand your brand's core values, mission, and vision. What makes your brand unique? What sets you apart from your competitors? Answering these questions helps you develop a story that aligns with your business goals and resonates with your audience.

Let's dive into some key aspects you should consider:

1. **Core Values:** What principles guide your business? These values should be evident in every aspect of your brand story. For example, if sustainability is a core value, your story should highlight your efforts to be environmentally friendly.

2. **Mission and Vision:** What is your business trying to achieve? Your mission and vision statements are the backbone of your brand story. They should inspire and motivate not just your audience, but your team as well.

3. **Unique Selling Proposition (USP):** What makes your product or service stand out? Your USP should be woven into your brand story, demonstrating

why customers should choose you over your competitors.

Knowing Your Audience

Understanding your target audience is crucial. Who are they? What do they care about? What motivates them? Your brand story should speak to their needs and desires, connecting with them on an emotional level.

Here's how to get to know your audience better:

1. **Demographics and Psychographics:** Start by identifying the basic demographics of your audience, such as age, gender, income, and education. Then, delve into psychographics – their interests, values, and lifestyle. This helps you create a detailed picture of who your customers are.

2. **Customer Personas:** Develop detailed customer personas. These fictional characters represent different segments of your audience. Give them names, backgrounds, and characteristics to make them more real. This helps you tailor your story to resonate with different types of customers.

3. **Feedback and Surveys:** Don't guess what your audience wants – ask them! Use surveys, feedback forms, and social media interactions to gather insights. What do they love about your brand? What do they wish you did differently? Use this information to refine your story.

Telling Your Story

With a clear understanding of your brand and audience, it's time to tell your story. Use language and visuals that resonate, creating a narrative that is memorable, engaging, and emotionally impactful.

Here are some tips to make your story stand out:

1. **Be Authentic:** Authenticity is key. Don't try to be something you're not. Your audience can sense when you're not being genuine. Share the real story behind your brand – the challenges, the triumphs, and everything in between.

2. **Use Relatable Characters:** People connect with stories through characters. Use relatable characters that your audience can identify with. This could be the founder of the company, an

employee, or even a customer. Share their journeys and experiences.

3. **Create a Narrative Arc:** Every great story has a beginning, middle, and end. Your brand story should follow a similar structure. Start with the problem or need that your brand addresses, describe the journey and the solutions you provide, and end with the impact on your customers' lives.

4. **Incorporate Visuals:** Visuals are a powerful storytelling tool. Use images, videos, and infographics to complement your narrative. Visual content is more engaging and can convey emotions and messages more effectively than words alone.

The Impact of Brand Storytelling

The power of brand storytelling is undeniable. When done right, it differentiates your business, builds an emotional connection with your audience, and drives engagement and sales. Start crafting your brand story today, and watch as your business becomes more memorable, meaningful, and successful.

Let's look at some real-world examples of how effective storytelling can transform a brand:

1. **Apple's "Think Different" Campaign:** Apple's iconic campaign celebrated creativity and innovation through emotionally powerful ads. By highlighting the stories of individuals who dared to think differently, Apple positioned itself as a brand that champions originality and progress.

2. **Nike's "Just Do It" Campaign:** Nike's campaign is one of the most successful branding stories of all time. The simple tagline and powerful visuals inspired millions to take action and achieve their dreams. Nike's story is all about empowerment and perseverance.

3. **Coca-Cola's "Share a Coke" Campaign:** Coca-Cola's campaign created a story of connection, friendship, and happiness by encouraging customers to share a Coke with friends and loved ones. This campaign resonated globally, making people feel part of a larger community.

Magnetic Storytelling: Engaging and Inspiring

In a world overflowing with information, capturing and keeping attention is challenging. But an engaging, memorable, and emotionally resonant story can connect with people and leave a lasting impact.

This e-book will guide you through the art of magnetic storytelling, providing tools and techniques to craft compelling stories that engage and inspire.

Key Components of Magnetic Storytelling

1. **Definition and Importance:**
   - Understand why storytelling is crucial in today's world.
   - Learn the benefits of telling compelling stories.
2. **Understanding Your Audience:**
   - Identify your target audience.
   - Understand their needs and desires.
   - Connect with them on an emotional level.
3. **Building a Compelling Story:**
   - Learn the elements of a great story.
   - Understand story structure and narrative arcs.
   - Craft relatable characters.
4. **Telling Your Story:**
   - Use appropriate language and tone.
   - Incorporate visual storytelling and images.
   - Use anecdotes and personal experiences.
5. **Bringing Your Story to Life:**

- ☒ Integrate your story into all aspects of your business.
- ☒ Maintain consistency in your brand message.
- Make your story relevant and personal.

6. **Power of Storytelling:**
   - ☒ Use storytelling in your marketing campaigns.
   - ☒ Build emotional connections with customers.
   - ☒ Drive engagement and sales with a magnetic story.

Expanding on Real-World Examples

Let's dive deeper into some examples to understand how powerful storytelling can be:

1. **Apple's "Think Different" Campaign:** This campaign didn't just celebrate creativity; it honored the spirit of innovation. Apple highlighted icons like Albert Einstein, Mahatma Gandhi, and Martin Luther King Jr., aligning the brand with these visionary figures. This not only positioned Apple as a leader in innovation but also created an emotional resonance with customers who saw themselves as part of a larger movement of changemakers.

2. **Nike's "Just Do It" Campaign:** Beyond the slogan, Nike used powerful narratives of athletes overcoming obstacles. Stories of everyday people achieving extraordinary things became central to the brand's identity. This approach made Nike's message of perseverance and determination relatable to a wide audience, from professional athletes to casual runners.

3. **Coca-Cola's "Share a Coke" Campaign:** By personalizing bottles with names and encouraging sharing, Coca-Cola tapped into the human desire for connection and recognition. The campaign's success lay in its ability to make each customer feel special and part of a global community of Coke lovers.

Magnetic storytelling is a crucial component of modern marketing and branding. By telling engaging, memorable, and emotionally resonant stories, you can connect with your audience and build lasting relationships. Whether you're a seasoned marketer or just starting out, these tips and tricks will help you craft magnetic stories that engage, inspire, and drive results for your business.

Next Steps

Now that you understand magnetic storytelling, it's time to put what you've learned into practice. Here are a few tips:

1. **Practice:** Start small and work your way up to more complex stories. The more you practice, the better you'll become.

2. **Get Feedback:** Seek opinions from friends, colleagues, or mentors. Constructive feedback is invaluable for honing your storytelling skills.

3. **Experiment:** Try different formats, styles, and techniques. See what resonates best with your audience.

4. **Stay Inspired:** Keep your creative juices flowing by consuming different forms of media – books, movies, podcasts, and storytelling events.

5. **Collaborate:** Work with other storytellers and marketers to share ideas and techniques.

Collaboration can lead to innovative storytelling approaches.

Magnetic storytelling is an essential skill for building a successful brand or business. Start practicing today, and see the power of magnetic storytelling for yourself!

In this book, we've explored the art of magnetic storytelling and its power in connecting with audiences and building successful brands. Keep practicing and experimenting. Find what works for you and your audience, and keep refining your skills. Whether you're a seasoned pro or just starting out, there's always room to grow and improve as a storyteller.

I hope this ebook inspires and empowers you to become a master of magnetic storytelling. Use your new skills to engage, inspire, and captivate your audience, and watch your brand soar to new heights!

Interactive Storytelling: The Future of Engagement

As we look to the future, interactive storytelling is becoming increasingly popular. People crave experiences that allow them to shape the story and have a say in the outcome. Imagine creating a brand story where your audience can choose the path, make decisions, and see different endings. This level of engagement can significantly deepen the connection between your brand and your customers.

Leveraging Social Media for Storytelling

Social media is already a powerful tool for telling stories and connecting with audiences. As these platforms continue to evolve, they will offer even more opportunities for storytellers to reach and engage their audiences. Think of Instagram stories, Facebook live sessions, and TikTok videos – these are all modern avenues to tell your brand's story in a dynamic and interactive way.

The Role of Technology in Storytelling

New technologies like virtual reality (VR) and augmented reality (AR) are opening up exciting possibilities for brand storytelling. Imagine immersing your audience in a virtual world where they can experience your brand story firsthand. These technologies can make your storytelling more engaging and memorable.

The future of magnetic storytelling is exciting and full of possibilities. With new technologies and innovative approaches, we can tell stories in ways we never thought possible. Embrace these trends and keep experimenting, and you'll be well on your way to becoming a master of magnetic storytelling!

By understanding your audience, crafting a compelling story, and bringing it to life, you can engage and inspire your customers and create a memorable brand experience. Use the techniques and tools outlined in this e-book to start telling magnetic stories that capture and keep people's attention.

I hope this ebook has inspired and empowered you to become a master of magnetic storytelling. Use your new skills to engage, inspire, and captivate your audience, and watch your brand soar to new heights!

4

Name Matters

"A good name is preferable to great riches,

and loving favor to silver and gold."

~Proverb 22:1

This verse from the book of Proverbs, written by King Solomon under the guidance of the Holy Spirit, speaks volumes. Solomon, considered one of the wisest men to ever live, was given the name Jedidiah by the prophet Nathan, which means "beloved of the Lord."

What does this ancient proverb have to do with King Solomon? Quite a lot, as it turns out. King Solomon's story is a testament to the value of a good name. In 1 Kings, Solomon is described as the wisest man who ever lived. After David's death, Solomon built the temple, which was considered the most magnificent building in the world at the time. In Ecclesiastes, Solomon reflects on his life, concluding that everything is meaningless except for one thing – fearing God and obeying His commands.

So, how did a man who started out with such humble beginnings become known as one of the wisest men on Earth? The answer lies in his name.

King Solomon was known for his wisdom and great riches. His name became synonymous with wisdom. But how did Solomon achieve such fame without YouTube, Google, Facebook, Instagram, or LinkedIn?

The most important lesson here is that a good name is more valuable than riches. It's far easier to achieve fame with a good name than with great wealth.

Solomon's fame grew after he became king, not just because of his wisdom but also because of his wealth and power. His name was known all over the world, illustrating how a good name can be more valuable than riches.

The story of King Solomon is a prime example of how a good name can be more valuable than riches. Solomon's name has been famous for a long time, conjuring thoughts of wisdom, wealth, and power. But why is this name so well known? And how can you apply Solomon's lessons to your own life?

The Bible is full of examples of people whose lives demonstrate that your character is connected to your name and that your attitude reflects the value you bring to your family, community, and marketplace. King Solomon is one such example. When Solomon became king, he asked God for wisdom to rule well (1 Kings 3:9).

The Lord was so pleased with Solomon's request that He not only granted him wisdom but also riches and honor (1 Kings 3:13).

Because Solomon had a heart for God, he used his influence to build up the people and nation of Israel.

As you read these excerpts from Proverbs, you will see that Solomon's name became famous not only because of his accomplishments but also because of his character. The story of King Solomon shows how his name became famous. You will discover the principles that made him successful and how you can apply them to your own life.

Have you ever wondered how King Solomon's name became famous? It wasn't because he was born into a wealthy family. It wasn't because he had a great education. And it wasn't because he held a powerful government position. No, King Solomon's fame came from his character.

Your name is connected to your character, and your attitude reflects the value you bring to your family, community, and marketplace. As King Solomon said, "A good name is more desirable than great riches; to be esteemed is better than silver or gold." (Proverbs 22:1).

When you think of the most successful businesses in the world, what comes to mind? Names like Google, Amazon, Tesla, Under Armour, and Apple probably top your list. But what do these businesses have in common?

Aside from being some of the most successful companies in history, they all have instantly recognizable names. But how do you choose a name for your business that will be both recognizable and successful?

It's not as easy as it seems.

Many businesses make the mistake of naming their company after themselves without considering the implications for their brand.

Your business name is one of the most important elements of your branding strategy. It's the first thing people see when they come across your business, and it leaves a lasting impression. Your company's name is one of its most valuable assets. If it's attractive and memorable, it can make all the difference in attracting customers and building a successful business.

Let's take a closer look at the power of a brand name and how to create one that will help your business succeed.

The Importance of a Good Name

What comes to mind when you hear these brand names: Nike, CocaCola, Apple, and Tesla? These names evoke positive emotions and associations. They are instantly recognizable and evoke feelings of trust, quality, and reliability.

A strong brand name is one of the most valuable assets a company can have. It can help attract new customers, increase sales, and build a loyal customer base.

It has been famously said that a good name is more desirable than great riches. This sentiment is true for individuals and is especially important for businesses. A strong brand name can make all the difference in the world for a business, no matter how big or small.

A good brand name creates an instant connection with customers, making them feel something and evoking an emotion. A name customers can trust and feel comfortable with is crucial.

We'll discuss how to create a powerful brand name and how to use it to connect with your customers. We'll also look at famous brands and see how they've used branding to become successful.

When it comes to branding, there are a few key things to keep in mind. The most important is to make sure your brand name is memorable and distinctive. It needs to be something people will remember and associate with your company. Additionally, you'll want to ensure your brand name is legally protected so that no one can steal it or use it without your permission.

Consistency in branding is crucial across all channels. When you hear the word brand, what comes to mind? Most people think of wellknown brands like Nike, Apple, Coca-Cola, and Pepsi. But branding isn't just for multi-million-dollar corporations. Your brand is one of the most important elements of your business and can mean the difference between success and failure.

What's in a name? Quite a lot. Your company's name is one of the most important decisions you make. It's connected to your success, your branding, and how you're perceived by your customers.

It has been famously said that a good name is better than riches. Your name is everything when it comes to branding. It's the first thing people see and the last thing they remember. It's the foundation of your marketing efforts, and a strong name can make or break your business. You should know how to choose the right name for your business and ensure it connects with your target audience.

We'll also discuss the importance of brand names and how they help your business succeed. When it comes to branding, your company's name is critical. It's one of the most important aspects of your business. Your name is the first impression potential customers will have, and it's the foundation upon which all other marketing efforts are built.

A good company name can help you attract new customers, create brand recognition, and differentiate yourself from your competitors. So, take your time to build and be ready to defend it. A good name can be the gateway to success. So, how do you go about selecting a good name for your business? And once you have a name, how can you make sure it contributes to your success?

Let's explore the important connection between your brand name and your success.

You have probably heard the old saying, "You can't judge a book by its cover." This is especially true for branding. Your brand name is one of the most important aspects of your business, but it is not the only thing that matters. A good name helps you attract customers, but a bad name can drive them away.

It is important to know your brand name and how it is connected to your success. We will also provide tips for choosing a good brand name and examples of brands that have successfully built their businesses around their names.

Seven years ago, I was working in Baltimore, MD, for one of the major athletic sportswear, footwear, and clothing brands in the world. Making $10.00 per hour, I learned many things about outsourced apparel, accessories, and footwear from countries like Cambodia, China, Taiwan, Vietnam, and Colombia. But all were labeled under one name: "Under Armour." The shoes, clothes, apparel, and accessories were not different from other companies, but this company stood out because of its meaningful, short, and attractive name, coupled with an amazing slogan that resonated in the athletic industry.

Before even marketing its product, this name was known worldwide, competing with giant sports brands like Nike and Adidas. This was because the name had a unique, stunning, and beautiful sound.

According to the Holy Scripture (Bible), a name is as spiritual as money. So, don't neglect it. For example, God gave the Israelites the principle of giving their children good names related to good character, honor, and authority, so they could glorify Him through these qualities. He changed the names of His people to empower their characters, beliefs, and spirits. From Abram to Abraham, and Jacob to Israel, these changes brought glory and honor to His chosen nation.

In John Chapter 1:1, it says, "In the beginning was the Word, and the Word was with God, and the Word was God. In Him was life, and that life was the light of men." Does your brand's name seduce people or bring light to your prospects, clients, or audience? Think carefully before choosing it. It may sound fancy, short, sweet, and powerful, but make sure it reflects truth and positivity.

John 1:14 continues, "The Word became flesh and made His dwelling among us. We have seen His glory, the glory of the one and only Son, who came from the Father, full of grace and truth." Does your brand name have a tangible meaning that brings solutions, empowerment, change, or elevates people's lives uniquely? Does it solve problems so effectively that your clients will remember it and dwell on it in the marketplace for a long time?

Your business and brand name should reflect your uniqueness. How are you connected to the truth that yourself, your business, and your brand keep the meaning of who and what you claim to be, do, and offer?

In short, what is your brand's name? What does it mean? How easily does it convey a clear message?

Are you keeping your word? Your business should have a beautiful name that honors your brand and sounds authoritative. A name is a major differentiator in all human activities, business, and life. This is why names and signs hold our identity, especially in our culture, business, faith, and character.

Take Under Armour's slogan: "Innovative, Motivated Human." These three words capture the essence of the brand. I remember stepping off the bus at Prince George's Plaza in Maryland, intending to buy shoes. I saw a mob of young adults, male and female, flocking into a store. Looking up, I saw the Nike Air logo. This brand attracted a large crowd, illustrating the power of a great brand name.

Price Matters

When it comes to differentiation, your price matters too. What kind of product or service do you bring to the marketplace? People might doubt its value if it's priced too low, questioning why it's cheaper despite the bigger problem and pain it addresses.

I'm not suggesting selling low-quality products at high prices. The greater the hardship and pain, the higher the price should match. Think about how efficiently and quickly you can solve the challenge. When you are cheap, nobody will believe in your value. Conversely, delivering low value at a high price destroys trust. Proverbs 11:1 says, "A false balance is an abomination to the Lord, but a just weight is His delight."

Understand the level of value you provide. High-class solutions for high-level pain should come at a premium price. Low value for a low price. Always consider the time it will take to deliver the solution because time is more valuable than money. The adage "time is money" is misleading. Time is a divine material, not human, and should be used wisely.

For example, governments can recover financially by printing more money, but lost time is irreplaceable. Don't trade your time for money.

You'll see this discussed further in the following chapters.

5

Value Creation Matters

First of all, know that "The Word" means Jesus Christ, the Messiah, according to John 1:1: "In the beginning was the Word, and the Word was with God, and the Word was God." Verse 3 shows us that all things were made by Him (The Lord Christ), as testified by the 14th verse that says: "And the Word was made flesh, and dwelt among us, and we beheld His glory, the glory as of the only begotten of the Father."

In God's business plan, He always starts with thoughts, planning, then communication into existence. Next, He organizes everything in perfect order, and finally, He implements tangible things in the flesh and refines them. This process reflects His true image and character. We humans often reverse the process, which is why many of us fail to provide value, leading to poverty. God, the Creator, categorized His creations into two groups:

1. **The creatures of Heaven & Earth:** These were created in the first six days simply by speaking, as recorded in Genesis 1:1: "In the beginning, God created Heaven and Earth." In verse 3, it says, "And God said, Let there be light, and there was light..."

2. **Creators, male & female:** In Genesis 1:26, it reads: "Let us make man in our image, after our likeness." This implies that mankind should use the same process to produce values that help lead people away from pain or towards solutions to satisfy and fulfill needs. The blueprint for creation and growth starts with God's design.

By thinking positively about your creation or business, speaking it into existence by organizing it correctly, and then turning words into tangible, physical things, you follow God's blueprint. Don't forget to multiply your output to have a significant impact and dominance in the market.

The first commandment says: "And God blessed them, and God said unto them, 'Be fruitful, and multiply; replenish the earth, and subdue it: and have dominion over the fish of the sea, the birds of the air, and every living thing that moves on the earth.'" This commandment instructs you to start your business by being who you are, with your identity as a foundation for building your character.

This rule is BE > DO > HAVE.

BE: Be fruitful - Develop a character and attitude that shapes your identity and prepares you to get your hands dirty. It's simple to produce if you embrace the role of a producer. Your attitude reveals your

identity.

More than that, you want to defend and protect your claimed identity by getting your hands dirty and beginning to shape information into things. Jesus Christ demonstrated this level of creation on the sixth day of the first week (Friday) by forming Adam before breathing life into his nostrils, making him a living soul.

Achieve a level of mastery so you can operate with ease. Build a system that overcomes challenges before they disrupt you. After discussing plans and desires, and doing the work, people will trust you to provide great solutions and fulfillment through your products or services.

1 Thessalonians 4:11-12 says: "And that ye study to be quiet, and to do your own business, and to work with your own hands, as we commanded you; That ye may walk honestly toward them that are without, and that ye may have lack of nothing." For years, many pastors and believers have misunderstood these verses, failing to produce things that could solve problems in their communities and ministries.

As a result, the Gospel's reach has been limited, and the body of Jesus has suffered from poverty due to a lack of knowledge and truth.

But it's not too late if you're still alive. God never takes away your gift or talent. He wants you to create solutions for problems brought by the enemy of darkness and serve others through your gift of wisdom and talent before you return home (Heaven).

Because He instilled in us a desire to do good and great things, He is glorified through our creations. Dominion means achieving a level of leadership and guidance for your clients or people in need of your products or services.

The Process of Value Creation

Having a positive attitude shapes your character, and there's a promise in the universe that the results of your efforts are guaranteed by the Creator. The word 'Word' means the spiritual material that Jesus Christ used to create heaven and earth by speaking them into existence.

The same breath He used to speak things into existence, He gave us so we can live.

Now, you can use your words to speak things into existence, elevate, encourage, or shape your clients' or community members' characters and get rewarded, whether in money, promotion, or other forms.

These verses show the secret behind mastering good words/speech that lead to a great and wealthy life. Proverbs is a unique book that instructs how to use good words to solve internal and external problems and bring solutions, earning rewards from God and His people. Words lead to wealth or death depending on how wisely and aware you are of their spiritual impact on the human soul.

Proverbs 18:20: "A man's belly shall be satisfied with the fruit of his mouth, and with the increase of his lips shall he be filled." Here are some tips for improving your speech habits if you're struggling to speak in ways that make others feel valued and important:

1. Speak positively and encouragingly: Guide and empower your clients to focus on their problems, not themselves, and become heroes.

2. Use phrases like "you're great" or "you're doing great."

3. Speak slowly and clearly: This gives others time to understand what you're saying.

4. Avoid critical or judgmental speech: This only makes people feel unvalued or unimportant.

5. Limit talking about yourself: This helps others feel like the most important part of the conversation.

6. Use body language effectively: Sit up straight, pay attention to your posture, keep your hands and arms relaxed, and make eye contact.

7. Practice saying "yes" and "no" effectively: This helps identify when you're speaking in ways that aren't helpful.

If you struggle to speak in ways that make others feel valued and important, consider seeing a professional counselor or therapist. They can help you understand why you're struggling and improve your speech habits.

When you speak, be yourself. Speak from your heart, and don't be afraid to be vulnerable or express your feelings. Being yourself makes others feel comfortable and valued, and it helps you communicate more effectively.

Remember, every person has value. Express this value in your speech, even when you don't feel like you're saying anything special. This builds good relationships and makes a positive impact on the world.

Take heart! You're on your way to speaking like a Proverbs-level speaker. Keep at it, and you'll be well on your way to success.

Power of Words

Proverbs 12:14: "A man will be satisfied with good if he is careful with his words and actions." This means a man will be satisfied with good if he is careful with his words and actions. You also understand that a man will be repaid according to his deeds. Therefore, let us be mindful of our words and deeds, so we may be satisfied with good and receive favorable recompense.

Proverbs 12:15-16: "The words of the wise are as goads, and as nails driven into wood: whereas the words of the foolish are as seeds dropped into the earth." This proverb warns about the evil that comes from bad speech. Solomon says that sin will bring destruction and suffering both to the person who commits it and to those around them. The souls of those who do wrong will be destroyed by their own violence.

This is a strong warning about the consequences of bad talk. You should not talk badly about people or yourself. Use your words wisely to avoid causing trouble for yourself or others. Speak for healing, motivating, and not hurting. When it comes to warnings, an evildoer might feel discriminated against or undermined, even if their soul and spirit know the truth.

If you want to enjoy a good life, be careful what you say. The souls of those who do wrong will be destroyed by their own violence. People will either absorb the message and change their lives or ignore it and move on. Your words are super important.

Using the Right Words

It's all about the power of positivity and the impact you can have on your audience. You need to use the right words to get your message across. We'll help you choose the best words for your marketing and advertising campaigns.

Use "Heartcore" words to drive traffic and clicks. If you're marketing your business, start calling your prospects by their names and positions or identities they qualify themselves as. Make sure your terms are automatically connected to your marketing system.

If they want to be marketers, they need to call themselves marketers from the start. The Bible says, "Man thinks, man becomes." Our tongue can be a blessing or a curse depending on how we use it. Instead of using the term "marketer," try "advertising" or "marketing professionals."

Always refer to yourself as a marketer to make people aware that you're marketing your business as a foundation of your business and life. The power within your words lets God speak into existence to create faith in you that chases doubt away. Belief can manifest from thoughts to words and words to things.

Examples and Stories of Value Creation

Let's delve deeper into real-world examples and stories that illustrate the power of value creation and the impact of a good name:

1. **The Story of Apple:** Apple started in a garage, founded by Steve Jobs, Steve Wozniak, and Ronald Wayne. They had a vision to create personal computers that were user-friendly and accessible. The name "Apple" was chosen because it was simple, fun, and approachable. Their commitment to quality and innovation, paired with their distinctive branding, has made Apple a household name. From the iPhone to the MacBook, Apple's products are known for their sleek design and cutting-edge technology. Their story demonstrates how a clear vision, consistent branding, and a commitment to quality can create immense value and build a loyal customer base.

2. **Tesla and Elon Musk's Vision:** Tesla, under the leadership of Elon Musk, has revolutionized the automobile industry with electric cars. The name

"Tesla" was inspired by Nikola Tesla, a pioneer in electrical engineering. Musk's vision was to create electric cars that were not only environmentally friendly but also high-performing and desirable. By focusing on innovation, sustainability, and cutting-edge technology, Tesla has created significant value in the automotive market. Their success shows the importance of a visionary leader and a strong brand name in driving value creation.

3. **Amazon's Customer-Centric Approach:** Jeff Bezos founded Amazon with the vision of being "the Earth's most customer-centric company." The name "Amazon" was chosen to reflect the vast selection of books initially offered, much like the Amazon River is vast. Over time, Amazon expanded to include a wide range of products and services. Their focus on customer satisfaction, convenience, and innovation has made them a leader in e-commerce. Amazon's success

highlights the importance of understanding and meeting customer needs in value creation.

Strategies for Effective Value Creation

To create value effectively, consider the following strategies:

1. **Understand Your Audience:** Knowing your audience is crucial. Conduct market research to understand their needs, preferences, and pain points. This information will help you tailor your products or services to meet their expectations.

2. **Innovate Continuously:** Innovation is key to staying relevant and competitive. Invest in research and development to improve your products and services continuously. Keep an eye on market trends and be open to new ideas and technologies.

3. **Build Strong Relationships:** Establish strong relationships with your customers, employees, and partners. Trust and loyalty are built through consistent and positive interactions. Provide

excellent customer service and create a positive work environment for your employees.

4. **Focus on Quality:** Quality should never be compromised. Highquality products and services create a positive reputation and encourage repeat business. Implement rigorous quality control measures to ensure your offerings meet the highest standards.

5. **Communicate Your Value:** Clearly communicate the value of your products or services to your customers. Use effective marketing and branding strategies to highlight the benefits and unique features of your offerings.

The Role of Leadership in Value Creation

Leadership plays a critical role in value creation. A strong leader sets the vision, motivates the team, and drives the organization toward its goals. Here are some qualities of effective leaders:

1. **Visionary Thinking:** A visionary leader has a clear and compelling vision for the future. They inspire

and motivate their team to work towards this vision.

2. **Decisiveness:** Effective leaders make informed decisions quickly and confidently. They analyze the available information, consider the potential outcomes, and take action.

3. **Empathy:** Empathy is the ability to understand and share the feelings of others. Empathetic leaders build strong relationships with their team and create a supportive work environment.

4. **Adaptability:** The business environment is constantly changing. Effective leaders are adaptable and can navigate through uncertainty and change.

5. **Integrity:** Integrity is the quality of being honest and having strong moral principles. Leaders with integrity build trust and credibility with their team and stakeholders.

Case Study: Under Armour

Let's revisit the case of Under Armour, a brand that has made significant strides in the athletic industry. Under Armour was founded by Kevin Plank in 1996. The name "Under Armour" was chosen to reflect the idea of wearing performance-enhancing gear under traditional athletic uniforms.

Kevin Plank's vision was to create athletic wear that improved performance by keeping athletes cool, dry, and light. The company started with a single product, a moisture-wicking T-shirt, and has since expanded to a wide range of athletic apparel, footwear, and accessories.

Under Armour's success can be attributed to several factors:

1. **Innovation:** Under Armour constantly innovates to improve their products. They invest in research and development to create new materials and designs that enhance athletic performance.

2. **Brand Identity:** The brand name "Under Armour" and its distinctive logo are instantly recognizable. Their branding emphasizes strength,

performance, and resilience, resonating with athletes and fitness enthusiasts.

3. **Marketing Strategy:** Under Armour uses effective marketing strategies to promote their products. They collaborate with professional athletes and influencers to showcase the benefits of their gear. Their marketing campaigns are powerful and inspiring, reinforcing their brand message.

4. **Quality:** Under Armour products are known for their high quality and durability. They have built a reputation for providing gear that performs well under various conditions.

5. **Customer Focus:** Under Armour listens to their customers and adapts to their needs. They engage with their audience through social media and other channels to gather feedback and improve their offerings.

The Importance of Continuous Learning and Development

To create lasting value, continuous learning and development are essential. The business world is dynamic, and staying updated with the latest trends, technologies, and best practices is crucial. Here are some ways to ensure continuous learning and development:

1. **Attend Workshops and Conferences:** Participate in industry specific workshops and conferences to gain new insights and knowledge. These events provide opportunities to learn from experts and network with peers.

2. **Enroll in Online Courses:** Online courses offer flexibility and access to a wide range of topics. Platforms like Coursera, Udemy, and LinkedIn Learning provide courses on various subjects that can enhance your skills and knowledge.

3. **Read Books and Articles:** Reading books and articles related to your industry can provide valuable insights

and keep you informed about the latest developments. Make it a habit to read regularly.

4. **Join Professional Organizations:** Becoming a member of professional organizations can provide access to resources, training, and networking opportunities. These organizations often offer certifications and other development programs.

5. **Seek Mentorship:** Having a mentor can provide guidance, support, and valuable advice. A mentor can share their experiences and help you navigate challenges in your career or business.

Balancing Value Creation with Social Responsibility

Creating value goes beyond profits. It's about making a positive impact on society and the environment. Businesses have a responsibility to operate ethically and sustainably. Here are some ways to balance value creation with social responsibility:

1. **Sustainable Practices:** Implement sustainable practices in your operations. This includes reducing waste, conserving energy, and using eco-

friendly materials. Sustainability not only benefits the environment but also enhances your brand reputation.

2. **Ethical Sourcing:** Ensure that your products are sourced ethically. This involves working with suppliers who adhere to fair labor practices and environmental standards.

3. **Community Engagement:** Engage with your local community and contribute to social causes. This can include volunteering, supporting local initiatives, and making charitable donations.

4. **Employee Welfare:** Take care of your employees by providing a safe and healthy work environment, fair wages, and opportunities for growth and development. Happy and satisfied employees are more productive and contribute positively to the business.

5. **Transparency and Accountability:** Be transparent about your business practices and take accountability for your actions. This builds trust with your customers, employees, and stakeholders.

Conclusion: The Journey of Value Creation

Value creation is a continuous journey that requires dedication, innovation, and a commitment to excellence. By understanding your audience, focusing on quality, building strong relationships, and balancing social responsibility, you can create lasting value for your business and society.

Remember, the process of value creation is rooted in positive thinking, effective communication, and tangible actions. By following the principles of BE > DO > HAVE, you can build a successful business that not only meets the needs of your customers but also makes a positive impact on the world.

Keep learning, stay adaptable, and embrace the power of words to inspire and motivate. As you continue on your journey of value creation, remember the importance of a good name and the legacy you leave behind. Your efforts will not only bring success to your business but also contribute to a better and more prosperous world.

So, take the lessons from this chapter to heart, and start creating value today. Your journey of value creation is just beginning, and the possibilities are endless.

6

Story Science

Storytelling has the power to engage, influence, teach, and inspire listeners. If you're an entrepreneur, author, coach, consultant, speaker, owner, or content creator, mastering storytelling skills is essential for the heart of your business.

There's an amazing opportunity to tell your branding story, and everyone likes a powerful story because it moves them subconsciously from point A to B.

But science has delved deep into the power of storytelling. Here is how science has revealed a great discovery about storytelling.

In fact, our culture, especially in the digital world, often relies on building PowerPoint presentations with bullet points and slides. However, research has shown that these presentations often focus too much on the storyteller's life, business, or past experiences but lack relevance to the audience.

The brain processes information in two major parts, especially when an emotional story is well-told:

1. Comprehension, attention, problem-solving, emotional zone, concentration, judgment/decision, and intelligence.

2. Sequencing area, organization process of speech & language, comprehension, and impaired hearing.

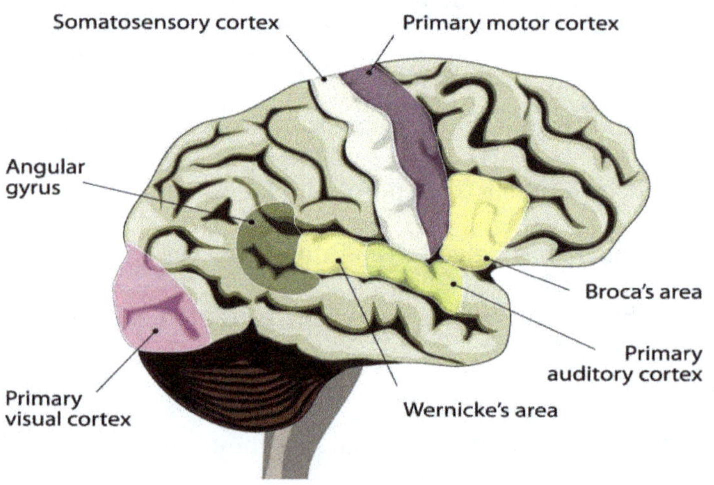

- ☒ Comprehension
- ☒ Attention
- ☒ Smelling
- ☒ Problem Resolving
- ☒ Emotional zone

- ☒ Concentration
- ☒ Judgment/Decision
- ☒ Intelligence
- ☒ Broken Words/Incoherent
- ☒ Speech.
- ☒ SEQUENCE AREA
- ☒ ORGANISATION
- ☒ PROCESS OF SPEECH
- ☒ &LANGUAGE
- ☒ COMPREHENSION
- ☒ IMPAIRED
- ☒ HEARING

However, when you speak and deliver truthful facts within a story, something else happens in the brain.

For instance, when a prospect enrolls in a talk session for a new club or mastermind, and you deliver a powerful presentation with real slides connected to a compelling story, their sensory cortex is activated, manifesting through smiles and the courage to assimilate the message.

So, the clearer the message, the more anticipation your audience will have to take action. Neuroscientists have found that when listening to a good story, the brain activates language areas and spreads information to other brain parts, preparing for a useful response.

Storytelling is not just about data; it's about engaging your audience emotionally and creating an impact. Here are 15 business benefits of storytelling:

1. Empathize with your audience.
2. Get people talking.
3. Motivate your team/members.
4. Increase your brand reputation.
5. Use storytelling to generate content ideas & build engagement with the audience.
6. Help your SEO.
7. Help your sales.
8. Help you avoid reputational risks.
9. Build loyalty.
10. Develop emotional intelligence.
11. Sell more services.
12. Get more traffic.
13. Generate more leads.
14. Grow your affiliate marketing.
15. Increase conversions.

"Wired for Story" by Leo Widrich discusses additional benefits of sharing stories in business and mentions, "Stories allow us to simulate intense experiences without having to actually live through them." Stories can be used in various settings to convey information, build relationships, and get buy-in on ideas.

Scientific discoveries have shown that dopamine is released in the brain when someone tells a story. This release helps create an emotional response in the listener, fostering a sense of connection, trust, and rapport between the storyteller and the listener. Ultimately, storytelling is a powerful tool that can shape emotions and responses, leading to positive experiences for both parties involved.

More importantly, oxytocin, a chemical released in the brain whenever a story is told, is associated with empathy, an important element in building, deepening, and maintaining good relationships.

Oxytocin is a pleasure-producing hormone released in response to other people's positive emotions, such as love and sexual desire. It is produced in the hypothalamus, a small brain structure buried in the posterior region of the brain. When oxytocin is released, it induces feelings of calmness and well-being, promoting social bonding and trust, making it the ideal hormone for creating lasting relationships.

In short, oxytocin is a natural love hormone that can help you build strong and lasting relationships.

Oxytocin is released when a person hears or experiences another person's emotions, such as fear, happiness, or sadness. The hormone is associated with empathy, crucial for building, deepening, and maintaining good relationships.

Oxytocin helps create a close connection between mother and baby during pregnancy and breastfeeding. This connection is crucial for the child's psychological development and later life. Additionally, oxytocin is involved in the female orgasm and in the production of milk for breastfeeding. So, telling good stories to pregnant or breastfeeding women is crucial.

However, oxytocin can also have side effects, including headaches, nausea, stomach pain, dry mouth, muscle spasms, dizziness, nervousness, dry eyes, heartburn, loss of appetite, sleepiness, sensitivity to light, anxiety, nightmares, erectile dysfunction, respiratory depression, fatigue, upset meditation function, loss of libido, restlessness, insomnia, increased anxiety, dizziness, and weight loss.

So, how can you release more oxytocin? Research has shown that activities like cuddling, hugging, building deeper and maintaining good relationships, meditation, deep breathing, and sexual activity help promote oxytocin release. Engaging in these activities will help you feel more in tune with your emotions, build stronger bonds with others, and make you more likely to trust them.

Most significantly, a story needs to make sense and have meaning. Stories are used by your mind to establish and analyze your own truths and beliefs, and to determine how you relate to the realities and beliefs of others.

Listening to stories gives you new perspectives and a greater understanding of your surroundings. Pose some questions to yourself and explore how others see the world through their eyes.

By sharing and listening to each other's stories, we all get a little bit closer to what's true.

Ultimately, storytelling is about the exchange of ideas and growth – and that's learning. Embedding storytelling in our organizational cultures and learning programs is essential. If you're trying to engage, influence, teach, or inspire others, you should be telling or listening to a story, and encouraging others to tell a story with you. You'll have plenty of science to back you up.

Be Careful Who You Listen To

Be cautious about whom you listen to because you may become a product of the stories you feed your ears, mind, and soul, especially when they come from a higher-level class or someone in a position of authority like a business mentor, consultant, guide, teacher, coach, speaker, expert, or partner.

Story Survey

Decades ago, I worked as an ethnographic research assistant with an amazing Ph.D. candidate from Columbia University in one of the largest refugee camps in the Western Tanganyika region. We interviewed and talked to hundreds of wise men and women from different countries, ethnic groups, tribes, languages, cultures, arts, and religions. Many of them looked the same.

I moved to the West to pursue my dream. While at Montgomery College in Silver Spring, MD, and the Rockville Campus of MD, I worked for one of the largest athletic clothing brands in the world, Under Armour. I traveled four hours to work in Baltimore, MD, for a 6-6 shift, then attended college for six hours.

One day, I fell asleep on a bus that took me to the station. I woke up, got on another bus thinking I was going home, but it took me to Downtown DC. When I woke up four hours later, I was lost.

That day, I should have been promoted, but my wife was pregnant, and I had my son's doctor's appointment. I chose to attend my son's appointment and lost my job two days later. This experience made me question the West, especially in the cold winter with a new climate, culture, and way of living. A new story was born. I heard God's voice say: "I created you to glorify Me as a human who is adaptable to any obstacles because your story is My glory."

Two weeks later, I got a door-to-door electrical bill contract in Washington, DC. I learned a lot about phone calling and direct response, earning a small commission per contract signed. I started questioning why 95% of people struggle with power bills in the richest country in the world.

Six months later, I moved to Tennessee and started learning about successful people and their stories of failure and success in various businesses and brands.

It took me three years of investing in myself, reading books like "Think and Grow Rich" by Napoleon Hill and "Rich Dad, Poor Dad" by Robert Kiyosaki. These books opened my eyes before I started learning about online business, which initially filled me with fear and a bad mindset about money as a

Christian. The power of the Gospel played a big part in my life. Blinded by false business examples that seemed evil, I discovered that few smart people made millions of dollars by providing needed products and services.

I took a leap of faith and enrolled in a digital business company. Everything seemed illuminating regarding email and Facebook marketing. One morning, at 9:00 AM Eastern Time, I opened my laptop.

BOOM! The message read, "CONGRATULATIONS THEOGENE NSANZE DAMAN, YOU MADE YOUR FIRST $1000.00 IN SALES." WOOOOOOOOOOOOOOW! This message filled my heart with immeasurable joy, and I started to celebrate. I called my coach, Mrs. Heather S., to let her know, and she congratulated me on making such an amazing amount in one day. I spent the next three days trying to nail all the systems to sell more and achieve even greater success.

But on the third day, before going to bed, I received a deceptive message stating that the company I was with was being sued by the FTC. They informed me that I no longer had access to any product or service and would be refunded within 30 days. What a tragedy! I cried, and my wife asked me what

79

was going on. When I told her, she simply said, "I told you that many people don't invest online." That was the last thing I needed to hear from her.

Thinking about the congratulatory message, my heart still tells me that if there is a fake dollar, there must be an original one. Without the original, the fake cannot exist. There is someone, somewhere, doing great things. I went back to work to earn real money and invest in higher programs by watching those who were in the same company. They invested a little bit in mentors and read the right books. I found people who were real but expensive, so I started with low-cost programs from people like Bob Proctor for mindset and Sam Ovens for becoming a business consultant.

Little by little, I attended live events, seminars, webinars, and workshops. I realized that all great leaders and legends across the past five millennia were great communicators. Think of Enoch, Noah, Abraham, Moses, Socrates, Jesus the Messiah, Josephus, J.F.K, Nelson Mandela, Clinton, and great entrepreneurs like Steve Jobs. Learning from a combination of their strategies, I was able to communicate at a higher level but needed a tangible proprietary process to serve my fellow leaders, coaches, consultants, speakers, and business mentors like Tony Robbins, Les Brown, Pete Vargas, and Pat Quinn, who are storytellers. Others included Jay Abraham, Roland Frasier, Myron Golden, Ph.D., Sam Ovens, and T. Harv Eker.

To achieve expertise in the subject, I spent three years with Pete Vargas, Pat Quinn, and their friends, nailing down and applying storytelling into the story-selling framework. This helped people connect and convert their strangers into subscribers and buying customers without spending a dime on ads or marketing.

Differentiate Yourself

There's too much noise out there. You can't just say to your audience, "Hey, look at me!" and expect them to listen.

Your audience is fickle; they only care about what's happening right now, not in the past or future. Forget about reaching folks on social media; it's not just you against your competitors but also your competitor's customers.

So, what can you do? People who use storytelling in their promotional material are more likely to:

1. Connect with your product on an emotional level, making them want it more.

2. Look at stories more than advertisements.
3. Build trust between customers and businesses when they share what is in it for the person listening or watching.

This means that storytelling is a good way to get customers interested in your business and can be a helpful marketing tool. Join me next time.

Tweet #smartstorytelling if you have any questions, comments, or concerns! See your story brand grow your business. This is how advertising used to be done before "there was an app for that." It's a way of reaching out to audiences by establishing trust through compelling stories.

Why Tell Stories? Isn't Branding Enough?

People don't connect with companies because they have a logo or an ad they saw once. They connect with people they trust. People you know in real life are part of your "tribe" – you feel kinship with them. You want to work with them, buy from them, and follow their lead. In the past, you were limited to whom you could reach out to when building connections.

The Experts Moves Podcast is a great example. It's a live show and podcast of discovery and growth in seven angles of human life where experts share their personal and business stories about their storms, pivots, peak impact, glory, legacy, and memorable moments.

Now, people can interact online, and it's easier to be part of a tribe that shares your beliefs and values. You no longer have one group you feel connected to – you can build connections with thousands through social media. And don't forget about print media; even though there aren't as many resources available anymore, they still exist, and your audience might prefer a newspaper or another source over scrolling down a Twitter feed.

If branding is all about getting attention, storytelling is about giving it – sharing something personal for others to connect with rather than being interested in what you're selling. Remember, storytelling is all about connecting with the audience you want to reach out to, unlike branding, which is more about getting attention and can be easily ignored by an audience, unlike storytelling.

The Art of Storytelling in Business

Many companies create good content, but few tell stories. They're in it for the big sale – the one-and-done. What would happen if you took a different approach? How much more effective could your business be if you shared good stories with your audience on social media and in print every day or week?

Storytelling can transform your business by building deeper connections with your audience, fostering trust, and creating a loyal customer base. By consistently sharing compelling stories, you can differentiate your brand, engage your audience, and drive long-term success.

Practical Steps to Master Storytelling

1. **Understand Your Audience:** Know who you're speaking to. Understand their needs, desires, and pain points. Tailor your stories to resonate with them on a personal level.

2. **Craft a Compelling Narrative:** A good story has a beginning, middle, and end. It introduces a conflict, builds tension, and resolves in a way that leaves the audience satisfied. Make your story relatable and authentic.

3. Use Emotional Triggers: Emotions drive action. Use your story to evoke feelings that inspire your

audience to take action, whether it's to buy a product, subscribe to a service, or support a cause.

4. **Incorporate Visuals:** Visual storytelling can enhance your narrative. Use images, videos, and other visual elements to bring your story to life and make it more engaging.

5. **Practice Consistency:** Consistency is key in storytelling. Keep your brand's voice and message consistent across all platforms. This helps build trust and recognition.

6. **Engage with Your Audience:** Encourage your audience to share their stories and engage with your content. This creates a sense of community and makes your audience feel valued and heard.

7. **Measure Impact:** Track the performance of your stories. Use analytics to understand what resonates with your audience and refine your storytelling strategy accordingly.

The Future of Storytelling

As technology continues to evolve, so will the ways we tell stories. Virtual reality (VR) and augmented reality (AR) are opening new possibilities for immersive storytelling experiences. Social media platforms are constantly introducing new features that allow for more creative storytelling.

Interactive storytelling, where the audience can influence the outcome of the story, is also gaining popularity. This type of storytelling can create a more engaging and personalized experience for the audience.

Incorporating these new technologies and approaches can enhance your storytelling and keep your audience engaged. Stay updated with the latest trends and be open to experimenting with new storytelling techniques.

Conclusion: The Power of Your Story

Storytelling is a powerful tool that can transform your business and personal brand. By mastering the art of storytelling, you can engage, influence, teach, and inspire your audience. Remember, it's not just about selling a product or service; it's about creating meaningful connections and leaving a lasting impact.

Your story has the power to inspire change, build trust, and drive success. Embrace the science of storytelling, understand your audience, and share your story authentically. As you continue on your storytelling journey, remember that the true power of your story lies in its ability to connect with others and create a positive impact.

So, take these lessons to heart, and start crafting your compelling story today. Your audience is waiting to hear from you, and your story has the potential to change lives. Keep learning, keep sharing, and watch as your story helps your brand soar to new heights.

7

Magnetic Story Selling

Crafting a persuasive, personalized elevator story for your audience is a fantastic method to establish trust by sharing something personal with them. People crave connection and can relate to stories more than information on a page or screen ever could. Once you have their attention, reveal what it is you're selling. If your story is interesting enough for people to stick around up until this point, they'll listen as you go on about the benefits of what's being sold and why they should buy it themselves.

By creating an experience through storytelling rather than immediately trying to sell something, customers will want the products more because they made a deeper connection with them and understand how it makes their lives better in some way. The key is to focus on your story first rather than trying to sell something right away. You'll need a good hook for people to get invested in the story you're telling, and then they will follow along as you reveal what it is about. In this way, storytelling becomes an experience—a way of sharing your point of view or vision for others to enjoy and benefit from. And don't forget that there's a difference between a great storyteller and a boring one—keep this in mind when drafting your own stories!

As a brand guide, we help business entrepreneurs, coaches, speakers, creators, and company owners share their message with the world through stories to grow their audience fearlessly and faster. To build a business that thrives, you need to understand the power of storytelling. All businesses have a story to tell. It's how they got started, why they do what they do, and what makes them unique from their competitors. The best brands can take their story and create something bigger than themselves.

"Storytelling is the way we explain the world around us, whether it's through our families, businesses, friends, or smartphones." Making it personal with stories about business successes in your industry or niche is a great way to help the audience connect. This builds trust and credibility so they know you can be trusted to provide them with good information on what you're discussing. Also, featuring people who have similar problems with your topics: how do you get customers? By implementing storytelling into the sales process, word-of-mouth marketing becomes even more effective, making it easier for others to recommend using stories as an effective way to promote products or services. By creating an experience through storytelling rather than immediately trying to sell something, customers will want the products more because they made a deeper connection with them and understand how it makes their lives better in some way.

The one subconscious thing that everyone does before they buy something is to look at reviews or read testimonials to see if the product they want to purchase will be worth the money. What would happen if you took a different approach? How much more effective could your business be if you shared a good story? People will follow along as you reveal what is in for them. Sharing stories of people who have benefited from using your service or product can create trust with customers who are looking into making a purchase, but it allows customers to connect on an emotional level rather than just reading facts about why they should use your business.

A lot of brands tell stories but few use storytelling properly. So how can you use storytelling to grow your business? What would happen if you took a different approach? How much more effective could your business be if you shared a good story? People will follow along as you reveal what is in for them.

But this doesn't mean they are not without downsides. People are focusing on sharing stories more on social media, which means the same story is told by many people, and it's less likely that people will pay attention to ads or look at something that isn't interesting. Using the storytelling method has the potential to backfire and put off customers because it takes longer than just telling them exactly what they need to hear: A lot of brands tell stories, but few are using storytelling properly. So how can you use storytelling to grow your business? What would happen if you took a different approach? How much more effective could your business be if you shared a good story?

What would happen if you took a different approach? How much more effective could your business be if you shared a good story? People will follow along as you reveal what is in for them. Sharing stories of people who have benefited from using your service or product can create trust with customers who are looking into making a purchase, but it allows customers to connect on an emotional level rather than just reading facts about why they should use your business.

Be Who You Are Meant to Be!

Change the story that's been told about yourself and tap into all its glory! This is your story. You are the main character and protagonist of it!

"You know what I mean when people say, 'it's about me?' Well, this isn't all about you; rather we're following one person on an adventure through life: ourselves."

What is the story behind your customer? The problem? The solution? The results? Fulfillment?

It's a wonder to think that we can't even touch the true depths of our being. But what if I told you, there were customers hidden in plain sight, just waiting for a service/product like yours? A product that knows how they live within themselves in pain, confused by the noise, shining light lost amongst all those shadows, wandering around aimlessly with no one else, and willing to give them eternal meaning, filled with the desire to tell their story.

Whether big or small - this could be about your customer! Your brand's life has value regardless of if others don't see how valuable you are right now. Remember: it takes work on our part for these mini tales (or whatever they may turn out like) to emerge from the dark, so please keep reading because everything starts at once...

The time to share your story is now.

Give voice with confidence and clarity, so that the world can hear what you have inside- all of it, including the good times as well as those hard moments when things got tough, or someone let you down (even yourself). When we know our stories on paper, we can live them through action; they become part of who we are in truth.

We all have a story to tell, but sometimes, the simplest details get lost in translation. Tap into your glory and let others hear what makes you unique— don't be afraid of how people might perceive or treat you because if they don't understand, there must not be anything special about yourself after all!

The Voice of a Lifetime

The power to be heard, seen, and understood by the world is inside each one of us – it's just waiting for you to attain the strength and courage to venture outside yourself and find your story. It takes guts because no matter how much time passes there'll always be more interesting stories out there than ours, but if we're willing to put our soul into telling them, maybe eventually people won't need anything new from any source whatsoever.

Story Selling Mastery

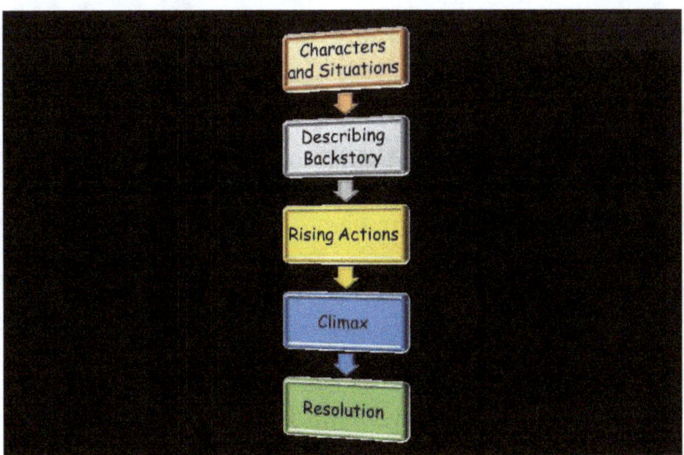

A person with great storytelling skills uses these three elements of persuasion known as humor (used simply because most humans find funny things more entertaining), and pathetic- the unique best way to engage an audience. It's more than just a storytelling device, it's what makes us human and connects us. When you share your story with others, they can see themselves in your shoes.

They can relate to you and feel like they're there with you on this journey of business ownership or entrepreneurship that we all go through at some point in our lives.

Storytelling is powerful and when done well will create a bond between you and your audience that lasts long after the conversation has ended.

What better way for me, who has gone through his struggles and triumphs over the years, to use my stories as a way of helping people find their own? I'm not telling other people's business stories instead.

Many people have a hard time telling stories without being bored. A story has a beginning, middle, and end. It's an interesting way to share information with your audience so they can relate their experiences in those same moments as you speak.

About them—or imagine what might have been! The traditional "plot" for stories follows a progression:

1. Setting up characters or situations
2. Exposition describing events before they happen (i.e., backstory)
3. Rising action when things start going badly but turn out okay anyway because sometimes it doesn't pay off if we give up hope at the outset
4. Climax/resolution where everything comes together
5. Resolution - We also see some turns away from classic storytelling norms like flash-forwards, allowing readers glimpses into future chapters without revealing anything crucial.

It is a cultural tradition that cannot be denied. From the earliest times, humans have been telling stories to entertain one another or pass on important knowledge from generation to generation. It's an art form within the roots of our society-but not just because of its entertainment value! Many different types of storytellers use their skills for purposes, such as teaching lessons about life and morals through tales passed down over generations. Every story has a different style. Learn to tell them in 3 ways!

Most of us are not very good at telling stories, but we all know that stories can be a powerful tool for motivating others.

Amplifying story branding is the best way to learn how to tell better stories in business and life. We've helped thousands of entrepreneurs improve their storytelling skills using our proven program. You'll learn how to craft compelling narratives that will motivate your audience and inspire them to act toward achieving their goals!

Most companies think they are using stories to connect with their customers, but most of them are not. The truth is that there's a big difference between telling your audience about your product and story and making an emotional connection that people will remember. When you use the right kind of storytelling, it can help you build stronger relationships with prospects, clients, employees, or anyone else who matters to your business.

The Bible is full of dramatic tales that center on conflict, relationships, and strong emotions. One such instance is the tale of King David and Bathsheba (2 Samuel 11–12), in which Bathsheba's husband dies as a result of David and Bathsheba's affair, and David's reign suffers as a result. We used to think that if we just posted the right amount of content and spent enough time on social media, customers would come flocking. But it didn't work out like that at all! Instead, we got frustrated and confused by an endless stream of posts and tweets that went nowhere fast.

Although the Bible is not typically associated with horror literature, there are a few passages that have supernatural, tense, and fear-inducing elements. One illustration is the narrative of the plagues of Egypt (Exodus 7–12), in which God unleashes a frightful series of punishments on the Egyptians in an effort to persuade Pharaoh to release the Israelites. Romance - The Bible is full of tales about love, passion, and the feelings that go along with it.

The Bible is full of tales about love, passion, and the feelings that go along with it. Ruth and Boaz's story (Ruth 2–4), in which a Moabite widow finds love and redemption in the fields of a wealthy Israelite landowner named Boaz, is one illustration.

In an epic tale, the focus is on bravery, adventure, and characters who are larger than life. The Bible is filled with many epic tales, including those of Samson, an Israelite judge who possessed superhuman strength, and Moses leading the Israelites out of slavery in Egypt (Exodus 1–14). (Judges 13-16). Characters and events in an allegory are used to symbolize deeper symbolic meanings or moral lessons.

Characters and events in an allegory are used to symbolize deeper symbolic meanings or moral lessons. The Parable of the Good Samaritan (Luke 10:25– 37), in which Jesus tells a tale about a traveler who is helped by a Samaritan, a member of a despised ethnic group, to illustrate the true meaning of neighborliness and compassion, is an illustration of an allegory in the Bible.

The Bible contains many tales that are set in particular historical eras and that reflect the social, political, and cultural climate of those times. One illustration is the Book of Esther, which tells the tale of a Jewish woman who ascends to the position of queen of Persia and uses it to protect her people from a plan to commit genocide.

In a prophetic story, God's message is expressed through a story or a vision. In the Book of Jonah, for instance, God orders Jonah to preach repentance to the inhabitants of Nineveh, but Jonah initially tries to avoid this duty. This is an illustration of a prophetic story. Jonah eventually understands the value of obedience and the reach of God's mercy through a series of supernatural occurrences.

The art of storytelling is a powerful tool that can be used to tell any type or length of story. There are various ways you could go about it, but the most important thing for writing in this genre would have been showing how each character's voice impacted their perspective on an event from the beginning until the end including all emotions and, details Depending on where you wanna take your audience or what kind of action you wanna them to take after your session.

A person with great storytelling skills uses humor, pathos, and logos in their works. its usually used as leading to an important point, which could be seen by some people to make others not believe what they are saying, but it also has another side effect of making someone want to find out more about something or remembering its context when hearing it mentioned later down the road.

Amplifying story brand is a powerful marketing strategy designed to increase acquisition & sales by creating meaningful connections through effective storytelling.

Our process helps businesses tell better stories so they can create more value for themselves and others.

We help our clients become better storytellers, so they can be more successful at attracting new customers without spending too much money on advertising or other marketing efforts.

Before we started using storytelling, our marketing campaigns were a mess.

Social media can be overwhelming – there's so much noise already! How are you supposed to stand out from the crowd? And how do you know what posts will resonate with your audience?

It's hard to tell who is paying attention anymore, and even harder still to get them excited about what you have going on. Plus, why should they care about your company anyway?

You've been around for years but haven't done anything exciting or interesting lately, so why should they pay attention now?

Business storytelling has been done wrong for a long time; we all know that entrepreneurs, business owners, and many leaders need to tell stories about their products and services, but most of the time, it doesn't work out well because we're not giving people a reason to care about what we have to say.

Old stories change the way business storytelling works by helping you create engaging content that gets people.

If the consumer is excited about your product or service, it generates more leads and conversions, meaning more revenue for your business! The old story about how to do business is harming your reality of business.

If you don't change this old story, it's going to hurt the present and future of you and your business.

Old stories are the biggest hurdle to your success. They keep you from seeing new possibilities and opportunities, which is why it's so important for you to know how to identify them and let go of them.

An old story can be a limiting belief that keeps you from achieving all you want in life. It might be a story about yourself or others around you, but either way, it will always hold some truth no matter how outdated it may seem.

Here's a better way to do things that will help you and your business in the present. The first step is recognizing what an old story looks like by identifying its key components as well as any potential triggers for those emotions associated with them. When we feel stuck, our natural response is fear – fear of failure, fear of change – these feelings come up because we're afraid of something going wrong if we do something different than what we've been doing before.

Once you recognize the emotion-stirring inside of you and acknowledge that there's nothing more to worry about other than making this chapter, you will identify the old business advice on how to get rid of them for good and create new compelling ones with clarity and high belief.

Most Businesses Still Use the Old-School Way of Telling Stories

They don't realize that it's possible to connect with people in a more meaningful and authentic way. There is a better way to tell your story, and we're here to show you how! A story helps create an amazing movement, business impact, and brings more revenue by using compelling customer stories that connect with their audience, generate leads, and build authority within their niche. Our mission is simple – help you build an online following by creating a compelling story that converts strangers into customers.

We are on a mission to help coaches, consultants, speakers, creators, owners, and experts to change the world of their business by storytelling through their blog posts, videos, eBooks & courses about creating powerful visual narratives for social media storytelling campaigns or generating leads for B2B companies. We've created tools like a signature talk, one–

liner, business mission, sales & marketing, message mastering, and stage mastering.

Story selling has been on the throne for more than six thousand years. Customers are constantly looking for better ways to understand your brand, so they can stay in truth within and trustable story framework. Many of the marketing techniques that have been used in the past are no longer effective. But story selling is the elevator for your customers and your brand.

The old school of your customers depending on old ways of marketing is dead, but this isn't necessarily a bad thing. It's time to embrace divine strategies that will help you grow your business and reach customers on a deeper level of connection and affection than ever.

Storytelling can be an incredibly powerful tool when it comes to connecting with your audience and engaging them on an emotional level. When you tell stories about how your products or services can improve people's lives, they're more likely to buy from you because they feel like they know and trust you as a brand.

Storytelling is a powerful tool for marketing and business. But it's also one of the most misunderstood tools out there. Many people think that storytelling can't be used to sell anything to anyone anywhere, but this isn't true. Well-told stories work in an authentic and relevant way to your audience's needs and interests.

Learn how to tell great stories about your company and products in a way that will resonate with customers and prospects who want to hear them. You'll discover what makes a story memorable and how you can use these techniques in social media posts, blogs, email newsletters, sales calls — even speeches at conferences!

Pivot Story Leads

Old Business stories are an issue for many companies because they are often hard to spot and even harder to eliminate. Many of these bad stories have been around so long that you don't even notice them anymore. But the damage they have created and continue to make is real. They create a culture where employees feel disempowered and confused about the ideal customer, the problem, and the solution which leads to low morale and high turnover rates, even procrastination and production or service shortage.

Most business owners who use these outdated techniques have fallen into the trap of thinking they're doing the right thing for their company, but they're just wasting time and money on things that no longer work.

This guide will help you stop following old marketing advice and start taking advantage of an amazing, powerful, and divine guide to growing your business faster than ever before.

You've invested in a lot of marketing and sales efforts, but you still don't see the results that you want. Your competitor is doing better than you are. It's frustrating when your message is not clear. It creates distrust, hesitancy, fear, unsubscribing, and or refund request. Your message through your personal story and your story brand are 2 legs to drive a truthful, profitable, and growing faster audience.

For each step, anyone can follow along to change the old business stories and make them their own. You don't need experience with storytelling or copywriting before, just take these three easy stages

1. What story emotionally touched your life like your audience's? Tell it.
2. Move through the middle of the section of your plot to pivot the moment.
3. End on an upward trajectory by correcting any problems at hand if necessary.

So, the process of shaping your new identity starts with creating a compelling story. But what's the best way to do this? It all comes down to understanding how people think and behave. A strong emotional connection is needed for them to want something they don't need, which means you can use emotion-laden content marketing strategies like storytelling (to an extent) to get their attention.

By using these principles strategically, you can build up that desire. Your brand is not the story you tell about yourself. It's how your customers know who you are, what makes you different from your competitors, and why they should buy from you instead of someone else. The power to shape this story resides in one place - with you. If it's time for a change but has no idea where to start?, let us help! We'll work with you to create an engaging new identity that will make all the difference between success and failure. Visit our website at brandingstorymatters.com today!"

"Change your internal story, it changes your focus. A changed focus changes your actions, changed actions, changes your results.

This is a part that millions of entrepreneurs love to talk about, and here is where the major mistakes are done. It's not about talking about the Victory only as celebration while no one got a clue which forest or jungle you started with your success journey. Your Good works follow you and lead you to a tangible victory. So stand tall and talk about where you are now attractively so the mob can trust and follow the journey at 100% that they will reach your mountain because if you celebrated, they can too.

Spot Your Client Problem.

"I've been in the business of coaching, speaking, and consulting for several years. I have seen a lot of people come and go, but one thing remains constant: the customer always has a problem they are trying to solve." It is not about how to identify your customers' problems. I will show you how to identify them!

In this chapter, you discover how to identify the customer's problem, the pain, and the solutions you have available. We will also show you how to present this solution so that they are not seen as pushy or sales oriented. As a speaker, trainer, entrepreneur, expert, or owner of your own company, it can be difficult to know what your audience is looking for in terms of information on a subject matter. The more specific you are with your target market by identifying their problems and needs then the more likely they will connect with whatever solution you're offering them. So before writing any content ask yourself: who is my customer? What do they need? And what am I going to offer them that solves their problems?

The problem with discussing the psychology behind sales is that it's not a science. It can't be measured and has little to no data; it leaves us guessing about how to make the sale, but does anyone ever dare ask for help?

We will focus on spotting your prospects' problems so you can offer them solutions.

Do it to get ahead. The information will be applicable no matter what you're selling or offering as well as being helpful if you just want more clients in general. Get ready for some actionable tips!

"This is a tricky question! But I'll give it my best shot. I think the problem many people have when trying to identify their prospect's problem is that they focus too much on the "what" and not enough on the "why."

I wrote this with the intent of helping entrepreneurs whose "what" is what your prospects are asking for. The "why,"

However, in this chapter, we'll discuss how to identify the customer's problem and the solutions you have available. We will also show you how to present these solutions so that they are not seen as pushy or sales oriented. As a speaker, trainer, entrepreneur, expert, or owner of your own company, it can be difficult to know what your audience is looking for in terms of information on a subject matter.

The more specific you are with your target market by identifying their problems and needs then the more likely they will connect with whatever solution you're offering them. So before writing any content ask yourself:

1. Who is my customer?
2. What do they need?

3. What am I going to offer them that solves their problems? Pretend to be like someone 'What' matters most in helping you understand how you can help them fix their problem. For example:

    What: the client wants to know if we offer marketing services.

    Why: they need more traffic to their website so they can grow their audience and ultimately generate more revenue from selling products or subscriptions.

I'm sure you know that business is tough these days. There are so many things to do and learn, it's hard to keep up with everything. Most people have their hands full just running their company. The last thing they need is more work on top of all the other duties they have. Often, we do most of our prospecting for new clients by phone or email, only meeting with prospects in person if we're lucky enough to be invited into a prospect's office for a meeting or presentation.

Now what most people don't realize is that with today's technology, there are plenty of ways to generate leads without having to make cold calls and sending out emails endlessly for high cost, but all these methods are useless if you don't understand your customer's problem, communicate their pain points language, show them your solution so you don't need a call to action.

1. Do you want to know the secret sauce? To identify your customer's problem framework? When you can identify their pain points, then they will be willing and more apt to buy from you. In this, we will teach you how to do just that! Let's get started!

2. First, how do you know if your customers have a problem? You can find out by asking them what their goal is and then asking if they feel that the current situation is working to achieve it.

3. Second, ask "what would happen if I didn't fix this?" This question gives them a sense of urgency in solving their dilemma which helps drive them to make the purchase.

4. Lastly, take note of any words they use when describing their problems- this will give your

insight on how to market yourself or your product to them!

This amazing book was written with the intent of helping you, your brand, and your team.

If you want to succeed in improving customer service experiences, start speaking in the language of your customers. Storytelling is a unique marketing tool. It is also important for salespeople to talk more about business through the stories of customers, rather than selfpromoting their products and services.

The first thing you need to do if you want to improve your customer service success rate is to speak the language of your customers. "What does that mean?" You may ask yourself? What I am saying is that it's time for you to stop speaking in terms of market research data, product attributes, features, benefits, and all those things which are not turning on your buyers these days! You have got to start talking in customer language!

Successful marketers will tell you that this means knowing what makes their customers tick so they can communicate with them in terms of their interests and concerns. It's all about using the voice of your customers to make your marketing messages more effective.

Ask yourself: what kinds of words do you (or other people on your team) use? How would you describe what you do/sell/offer? Do those same terms show up when it comes to communicating with customers?

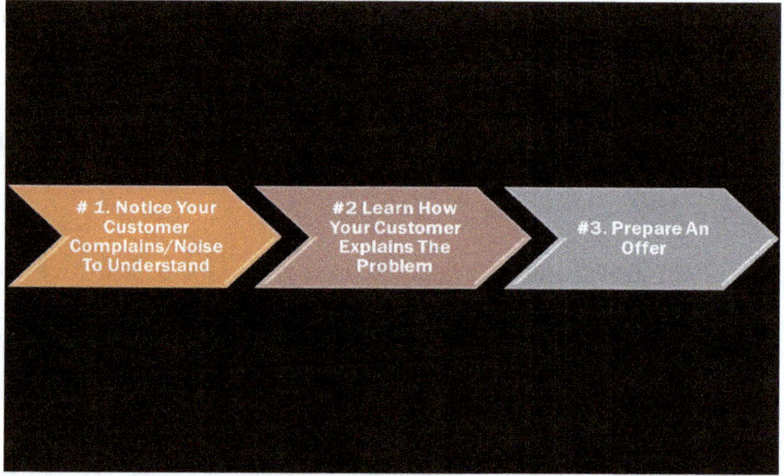

The first step is for marketers to stop extolling the virtues of products and services and start talking about how they solve problems—the problems that are important to their prospects. And then give them proof that the solution works by using a case story. It can also help if you talk about how much better life is after a purchase has been made, by using terms that focus on benefits rather than features.

Learn the language of your customer and always be prepared with an appropriate story or example that can help seal the deal. And keep in mind that all stories have a beginning, middle, and end so when you are telling them, structure them properly for maximum impact.

"Customers need always be happy with the product or service they receive. Customers want to feel like their concerns matter, but often feel ignored by companies that don't take the time to listen and understand them.

By using this customer language translator, you can speak in your customers' language, so they know you're listening and understand what matters most to them. This will help improve your business relationships with current customers, as well as attract new ones looking for a trustworthy company that cares about their needs.

We are all different, but many businesses forget this when they talk to their customers. Your company is unique, and your customers want to know that you understand them. They don't need a bunch of buzzwords or jargon. They just need someone who understands them and speaks their language.

Speaking in your customer's language will help you do exactly that. This book contains proven strategies for personalizing the way you speak with every customer, no matter what industry they're from or how big or small your business is! By using simple language techniques like "you" instead of "one", you'll be able to build trust with each one of your clients quickly!"

Business Pain Point + Direct Solution = Business Story

Ex: most people in marketing and sales are losing money in ads. We provide your 'story-matter' challenge on the story and stage experts keep a secret that is no longer a secret for everyone who has been blessed to get a copy of the power of your signature talk now or in the future.

1. Notice your customer complaints/noise to understand. What makes your customer wake up in the middle of the night? Pay attention to hearing what is the internal pain so you can address that from your heart, Analyze external pain so you can bring antidotes when you address them logically.

2. Learn how your customer explains the problem. Start practicing how your customer explains the

problem, step by step by talking to yourself if you got the customer's problem and pains, now it is the time and opportunity to communicate powerfully customer's language.

3. Prepare an offer. Get ready with whatever offer suits you because after you talk or speak to your customers standing in their shoes shows them fulfillment in the end, and they act like crazy to get that transformation to happen faster.

Branding Using a Story in 3 Categories

Big or small, a company's brand is the most asset. It's the single most important thing they do differently from their competitors. It can set you apart from those who sell similar products and those who want to buy them. Branded storytelling is the art of selling your branded product as an extension of your customer's story.

It's a way to increase sales and loyalty by showing the most assets. It's the single most important thing you do differently from your competitors. It can set you apart from those who sell similar products or services and those who want to buy from you.

Branded messaging is the art of selling your branded products/services as an extension of your customer's story.

It's a way to increase sales and loyalty by showing customers that you understand better than anyone else. One of the best ways to create a memorable story for your customers is through your high messaging, a long or short story that resonates with your customer. Problems in-depth show how the solution not only urgently can bring

transformation, but the feeling and look will be on a high level.

1. Explain your plan
2. Why you are qualified to do the work
3. How much it will cost and what they can expect from you
4. What the customer should expect from you as a business partner
5. Provide testimonials or referrals if they exist
6. List any other pertinent information

The episodic story is made up of a story sequence, story structure, and Story time. It is nothing without the location where the events unfold such as the story setting.

An episodic story's characters include a hero, heroine, nemesis, sidekick, and mentor. Episodic framework includes the settings and characters of the episodic story The story sequence includes story introduction, development, climax, and resolution. Episodic story structure consists of the episodic story framework of the content brief, which is known as an introductory hook, progressive complications, climactic showdown, and conclusive ending. It is a way you can make sure your audience remembers what you are teaching them by writing stories around it. An episodic story will not be forgotten because the audience will be entertained by the characters in a setting with conflict and tension, climax, and denouement".

8

Winning Talk Framework

The power of your signature talk can change lives in five minutes, three minutes, or even less. This chapter will explore everything you need to know about a signature talk and how it can help you become great at presenting tools in your sales & marketing, speaking, training, consulting, coaching business, or getting your message out to the world.

I'll share my story on how to use a signature talk after speaking with Peter.

He introduced me to his partner, so we started talking, and about this discussion, I needed to stop the conversation right at the beginning to answer some questions. Why do we listen to your speech or you in a speech?

It's very important in any presentation in communication; you must know where to start: take this person where they are if they're not interested when they are tired when they're having coffee when they are in the mood when they don't want to listen to me. Or when I'm not interested?

"What do I do and how do I do it?" That's where your customer lies. If you're getting rid of them before you start the conversation, it takes off because you're an awful speaker, who cannot sell themselves - a speaker who cannot tell a story and wants to get rid of him.

The first thing is you must understand how to start this conversation with your customer and get promoted yourself in the first two minutes.

Second, you must understand how to create a connection with the hero as a guide. The third thing is you must get your customer in alignment with your mission, vision, and values to help escape the world of victims and take the leap of victory. It's very important for any mission.

Critical business owners need this technique/tools or even skills to develop their business high message out there because I had difficulties when I went on LinkedIn with Victoria in a consulting call session three years ago.

I was silent, took a shot, and it took me 30 minutes to get out of my head and start speaking because for some reason the level of intimidation from people in a hustle makes people say, "it's okay, no problem"; but when you see your problems, nobody is going to solve those problems.

The reason those people (even those speakers from this summit) cannot do it is that they don't know how to do it. In my opinion, they don't understand the psychology behind the human brain's behavior in people, in their audience, and their customer's needs, and they don't match them nor their language or their mission/vision/values, so they cannot answer it.

It's very important you start this conversation with your customer in your first two seconds because once they heard what you say when you solve problems for them when you answer their questions, and when you're in alignment with them, they will buy, and immediately start promoting your business and your services by re-telling your business's products/service, brand, corporate company's story all over the online and offline stages.

You are going to use these next four main parts of your signature talk.

Most speakers, coaches, consultants, creators, owners, and experts are one-sided, they speak from the head. They use their intellect to persuade and influence an audience but never connect with them emotionally. This is a big problem because in today's fast-paced world people need more than just facts and figures; they want to be connected on an emotional level as well.

1. Opening Attitude (allow yourself to be vulnerable while you show your pit life)

2. Character (offer information that will help your audience make better decisions) by pointing on your pivot moments

3. Action Command (give them something specific that they can do immediately)

4. Closing Attitude Story (background information) by providing the foundation of your belief that your audience is looking to have.

People love sharing their stories, especially about failure, so share yours! Talk about a time when you thought everything was going well, but it went wrong. Do not be afraid to let them see who you are or what you don't know. The more vulnerable you are, the better.

The second tool is called head content; this one is essential when trying to persuade someone with facts and figures. If your audience does not understand your data, how can they implement it? Here are two ways to use content that will help them make better decisions.

First, you can talk about how your product or service helped another company out. Yes, I know this is a little tricky but if your audience believes in your brand, they are more likely to try it themselves.

Secondly, you can compare the prices of two different companies. This is very effective during a sale period, but you will need to have competitors in the same industry with similar products. The key is for you to tell your audience why yours is better even though it may cost more money or have fewer features.

The third tool is action hands; these are ideas that your audience can immediately take home to implement. They are small techniques that will help them solve a problem or improve their life.

For example, if you have a marketing service, tell them how to do marketing without spending money. If your product is aimed at children, give parents some fun things they can do with the kids.

These actionable suggestions should be something for them to immediately begin after the presentation.

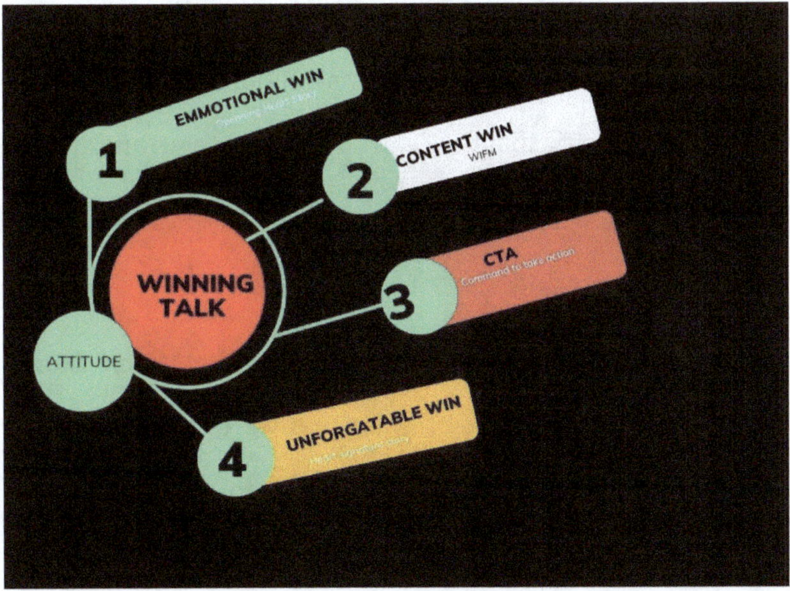

The fourth tool is called closing heart. You have put your heart out there throughout your presentation; now it is time to summarize what you said. If you said something funny, you could use that to get them excited about the next presentation which will only be better since they have new knowledge on.

Whatever topic you are giving a speech on. Tell them how they have changed as a person by listening to you or tell them how anyone can change the world if they just act. People love stories with great endings so make sure you give your audience one!

These tools: the open heart (allow yourself to be vulnerable), head content (offer information that will help your audience make better decisions), action hands (give them something specific that they can do immediately), and closing hands.

The Two Seconds One-Liner Framework

The best part about this story is agitation–problem–solution. Ex: "We hated it when we were in a hurry and couldn't find something in our purse to write on," This happened so often," we came up with an idea," "We started designing bags with built-in pen pockets!"

Here's a story of what we did and how we did it: We created an online program that reduces pain points by generating leads & improving customer service scores.

First, we analyzed the company's strengths and weaknesses to see what needed to be done.

Second, we conducted research using different types of customer surveys (and market research) to determine the best solution for them in their position.

Finally, we worked on a plan which included a detailed set of objectives for this year together with changes to strengthen internal systems and processes so they could reach their goals.

We can call them to tell their story -solution in 2 seconds only.

For more practical when it comes to mastering signature talk tactics, three frameworks and orders kind of information and call your signature talk if you can nail it down yourself, follow me on Instagram and Facebook on top housing on LinkedIn, and I'll be happy to work one-on-one and make sure you need on your signature turn off your story so you can reach your brand, your business, your company even your marriage saliva personal life and have that kind of story.

On Stages

Stages have been serving Kings and Queens, Palaces, and in Market Place for more than 4000 years. From Moses to Socrates to Jesus to M.L.K. Jr. to Tony Robbins to Club House, entrepreneurs, leaders, coaches, consultants, speakers, experts, and content creators are now struggling to get their message and offers out to the world so they can grow their impact and income. It's either because they've been taught that selling from the stage is icky, or they worry that they'll be perceived as a used car salesman.

Stages matter in the unique way of connecting and converting your message out of this world will help guide organizations with their mission by connecting them through stories told effectively across all channels so they too may reach more souls striving toward perfection in a time when the world is rapidly changing and people have become more connected than ever before, you need to be heard.

The unique way that Lisa Nichols can help your message stand out from all others has been proven in her successful career as an international speaker who connects with audiences on such personal levels, so they never forget what matters most! How you present yourself on stage can make all the difference in the world.

If you're nervous, your audience will sense it and they'll be less likely to enjoy the show. However, if you take the time to relax and focus on your performance, you'll be able to connect with your audience and give them an unforgettable experience.

The key is to remember that stage presence is just as important as talent. So next time you're getting ready to take the stage, make sure you're in the right mindset and that you're ready to give your all.

With a little preparation, you can make any stage your own. How you present yourself on stage matters. Your posture, your facial expressions, and even your clothing send nonverbal messages to your audience that can influence how they perceive your message.

For example, if you are giving a presentation on a new product, you will want to dress in a way that conveys confidence and professionalism.

On the other hand, if you are performing in a play, your costume choices can help to create a specific mood or atmosphere. In either case, it is important to be aware of the message that your appearance is sending.

By taking the time to thoughtfully consider your onstage persona, you can ensure that you are making the best possible impression on your audience. How you present yourself on stage matters.

If you're slouching, your audience will think you're bored or uninterested. If you make too much eye contact, they might feel like you're staring them down.

And if you pace back and forth, they might start to feel antsy themselves. So, what's the best way to command attention and keep your audience engaged?

First, take a deep breath and relax your shoulders. Then, try to make steady eye contact with individuals around the room.

And finally, stand still or take small, deliberate steps—any movement should serve a purpose. By following these simple tips, you'll be able to project confidence and control—two essential ingredients for success on stage. What you do on stage matters.

Every action, every word, and every movement matters. They all come together to create the experience that is your performance. And that experience is what your audience will remember long after the curtain falls. So, when you're on stage, give it your all.

Pour your heart and soul into your performance, and make sure that every moment counts. Only then will you be able to truly capture the magic of live theatre.

Having a powerful message or story to tell is crucial but being on the right stage or in the right room is even more important. In personal relationships or business transactions, we need to make sure that our audience is receptive to what we have to say.

If we're not communicating with the right people, our message will fall on deaf ears. That's why it's so important to do your research and make sure that you're talking to the right people about the right things.

Only then can you hope to achieve success in your communication attempts. What is more important in communication, having a powerful message or being in the right room? That is a difficult question to answer. Let's look at some of the factors that might influence the answer.

Why do you want to communicate? If you want to make a difference in the world, then a powerful message is probably more important. If you want to advance your career or sell your knowledge, then being in the right room is probably more important. What is your audience? A powerful message will probably have more impact on an emotionally receptive audience.

But if your audience is skeptical or uninterested, then being in the right room might be more important because it gives you a chance to build rapport and trust. In personal relationships, what is more important might depend on the situation.

If you are trying to resolve a conflict, then a powerful message might be more important.

If you are trying to build a deep connection, then being in the right room might be more important. As you can see, there is no easy answer to this question. It depends on your goals and your audience. But one thing is for sure: being in the right room won't matter if you don't, I'm not talking about the kind of stage that's made of wood and has a curtain. I'm talking about the stages we create in our lives. The places where we put on a show for other people to see. Our school, our jobs, our hobbies, and even our homes can be considered stages.

And just like in a real stage, we have control over what happens to them. We can decide what kind of show we want to put on. Some people are content to let someone else control their stage. They're happy to be background characters in someone else's play. But I think it's so much more powerful to create your stage. To be the star of your own life.

That way, you get to control the story. You get to decide what happens next. So, if you're not happy with the way your life is going, maybe it's time to create a new stage. A place where you are the star. It's time to take control of your life and write your own story. The power of the stage is yours for the taking. Go out there and create something amazing. Why should you use physical stages? I'll tell you why.

People like to see things in person; it's how we're wired. We like to meet the people we're going to do business with and get a feel for them. That's why physical stages can be so important. If you're trying to reach an audience, booking a physical stage can be a great way to make that happen. You can use physical stages to meet your audience, get their attention, and close the deal.

How? Well, first you need to find the right stage. Make sure it's in a good location and has the right amenities. Then, reach out to your potential audience and let them know you'll be there. Finally, follow up with them after the event and stay in touch. By using these steps, you can book a physical stage that will help you meet your audience and close more deals. There are many different stages that you can book to use for your performance or meeting. Each stage has its benefits that can help you better engage with your audience.

Here are some of the most popular stages and why they might be right for you: The first stage is an outdoor stage. This is a good choice if you want to be able to have a lot of people in attendance, as there is typically more space outdoors. Additionally, outdoor stages often have good acoustics, making it easier for your audience to hear you. Another option is an indoor stage. Indoor stages can be a good choice if you need more control over the environment, such as if you are doing a presentation that requires a specific temperature or level of lighting.

Additionally, indoor stages can often be more intimate, which can be beneficial if you want your audience to feel closer to you. Finally, you can also choose to use a mobile stage. Mobile stages are great if you need to be able to move around easily or if you are performing in multiple locations. Additionally, mobile stages can often be set up quickly and easily, which can be helpful if you are working for a limited amount of time.

The very difficult thing when it comes to booking those physical stages which sometimes are not in the local areas it takes a lot of energy time and money to get booked for free or paid speaking coaching or consulting even engagement or keynoting appointments setups, TEDx Talk Application it reams even harder for someone who never but passionate about sharing that great amazing message at the Greater and Highest Stage, Knowledge, wisdom ad tools are needed to help you Move to the next Stage,

Understanding, mastering if you like the Mind of a Meeting Planner with the real Philosophy of Positioning yourself with tangible testimonials and case studies of your why and how their stage matters and congruently Match the message and

the audience freely or paid values matter the most.

1. Contact the manager of the arena.
2. Send your request with proof.
3. Remind.
4. Send a reminder.
5. If agreed, send a kit.
6. Reach earlier.
7. Master the room.
8. Take a breath before you get on stage, be excited.

9

Offer Matters

You've worked hard to create an incredible deal for your clients, but it's just sitting there on your website, not getting the attention it deserves. It's frustrating, isn't it? But the good news is, there are simple steps you can follow to increase your digital offer's visibility and effectiveness. One of the most common methods to develop your email list and lead acquisition is through lead acquisition offers. These offers are great for establishing a rapport with your audience and obtaining their contact details.

Let's dive into the four most common forms of lead acquisition incentives: free reports, free samples, contests, and coupons. Each of these has its unique way of engaging potential clients and getting them interested in what you have to offer.

Free Reports

A free report is a sample of a larger product that you may use before making a purchasing decision. It's like getting a sneak peek into a book or a movie trailer. Reports are excellent for keeping your audience informed and interested. They help you stay on top of your thoughts and preserve a record of important details.

Imagine you're offering a comprehensive guide on digital marketing strategies. By providing a free report that highlights the key points, you give potential clients a taste of your expertise and the value you bring. It's a great way to build trust and showcase your knowledge. These reports can be crafted to address specific pain points or questions that your audience frequently has, making them highly relevant and useful.

Free Samples

Free samples allow you to test out new items before deciding whether to buy the full-size version. Think about it: how many times have you tried a free sample at a grocery store and ended up buying the product? It's a powerful marketing tool.

When companies give away free samples, it's not just about the product; it's about the experience. People love trying things for free, and if they like what they experience, they're more likely to make a purchase. Free samples help remove the risk from the equation and make it easier for people to say yes. For instance, if you're in the beauty industry, sending out free samples of a new skincare product can create buzz and encourage word-of-mouth recommendations.

Contests

Contests are a fun and interactive way to engage your audience. Who doesn't love the thrill of possibly winning something? Contests can generate excitement and buzz around your brand.

For example, you could run a social media contest where participants have to share a story about how your product or service has helped them. This not only creates engagement but also provides you with valuable testimonials and user-generated content. Contests can be as simple as asking users to tag friends, share posts, or create content related to your brand, increasing your visibility and reach.

Coupons

A coupon is a discount code that may be used to make a purchase. Coupons are frequently given out by companies to entice new consumers or reward existing ones who have remained loyal. With a little forethought, your firm can benefit from an effective discount promotion.

Tracking your coupons is crucial if you want to adjust and improve your campaign. Measure coupon performance through redemption rates or click-through rates. Customer feedback is also a good indicator of whether your coupon campaign is satisfying your clients. Effective coupon strategies can include limited-time offers, percentage discounts, or buy-one-get-one-free deals, all of which can drive urgency and spur purchases.

Free Tips #1: How to Develop a Branding Framework

Branding Discovery

Branding discovery is the first step. Understand how important branding is for your business and identify your brand's unique selling proposition (USP). Who influences your brand identity? How do you conduct branding and market research? And crucially, how do you maintain brand consistency?

Rebranding is essential for any business, big or small. It helps you stand out from competitors and connect with customers. However, without careful planning, it can be a time and money sink.

Creating a Branding Framework

A branding framework is a collection of standards that keep your branding activities on track. It should answer questions like "Whom are we attempting to reach?" and "What message do we want to send?"
Think of it as a guide.

For example, if you're a budding coach, consultant, speaker, content producer, or expert with a fantastic product or service, you need a branding framework. It's a holistic roadmap to market success. A strong branding strategy examines every encounter your customers or clients will have with your products or services and sets out how you want them to feel.

Finding Your Niche

To nail your niche, answer these three questions:

1. How does your product or service help your ideal customer?
2. Why should they purchase from you?
3. Where can you find them?

Niche firms that have raised sales fivefold in the past five years know how to pinpoint their niche. It's about finding a doorway. Entrepreneurs need branding to help customers understand what your firm sells and give you a competitive edge.

We're a full-service branding guide that can help you build a unique brand identity and reach your target audience. Your outstanding product might be unknown because you lack a strong brand. Your firm is invisible without it. We can help you establish a strong, memorable brand that stands out from the competition.

Messaging and Consistency

Branding goes beyond a name or logo. It's about your company's global image. This includes the website's design and how customer support answers the phone. A brand must express what a firm stands for and what sets it apart from the competition.

Effective branding involves preparation and execution. Branding helps create and promote a firm or product's identity. It requires strategy, the appropriate methods, and flawless execution. Branding can make even a modest firm appear big, while mistakes can confuse and repel clients.

Successful companies share key traits. They know who they are and what they desire. They design consistent messaging that communicates their distinctiveness to their target audience. Finally, they reaffirm their brand, which is more than a logo or product—it's an adventure.

Creating an engaging brand message is crucial. Your company's brand message should be clear, consistent, and unique. It should center on your target audience's demands and be communicated across all platforms, from your website to your commercials.

Developing a Strong Brand Message

Sometimes it's difficult to craft a strong brand message. Start with these tips:

1. Know your values. What differentiates your business?
2. Understand your audience. What do they need? How can you help?
3. Simplify. Your brand message should be brief and straightforward.
4. Consistency. Use your brand message consistently across all media.

Branding defines you. It's how consumers and prospects see you and the foundation for marketing. Creating a strong, consistent brand is key to attracting new consumers and growing your business. Your brand's message is what prospects should remember most about you.

Strategies for Effective Branding

Creating a brand involves giving the firm and its goods a memorable identity. Brand components include:

- Brand name
- Symbol
- Slogan
- Design palette

Mission, values, and target audience play a role in picking these elements. Branding encourages client loyalty. When people enjoy a brand, they're more inclined to use its products or services even when alternatives are accessible. Branding can help firms charge more for their products or services because buyers will pay more for superior quality.

Why Brand Products/Services?

Product branding makes your product easily distinguishable from competitors'. It's crucial for businesses that want to establish a strong presence in the marketplace. Branding gives a sense of professionalism and trustworthiness to a product, making it more appealing to potential customers.

Branding may also help you establish an emotional connection with your audience, making them more likely to purchase from you again in the future. Ultimately, product branding is about creating a distinct identity for your product that resonates with your target audience and sets you apart from the competition.

The Importance of Storytelling in Branding

A powerful way to enhance your branding strategy is through storytelling. People connect with stories because they are memorable and evoke emotions. When you tell the story of your brand, you give it personality and life. This connection makes your brand more relatable and engaging.

Consider sharing the journey of how your business started, the challenges you faced, and the milestones you achieved. This narrative can create a deeper bond with your audience. For instance, a fitness brand might share the founder's personal journey of overcoming health issues through exercise, which led to the creation of products designed to help others achieve their health goals.

Engaging Your Audience

Engagement is key to maintaining a strong brand presence. Social media platforms are excellent tools for interacting with your audience. Share your stories, respond to comments, and create content that encourages participation. Hosting live sessions, Q&A segments, or behind-the-scenes looks can make your audience feel more connected to your brand.

Additionally, user-generated content can be a powerful engagement tool. Encourage your customers to share their experiences with your products and services. Repost these stories on your social media channels to show appreciation and build community.

Measuring Your Branding Efforts

To ensure that your branding efforts are effective, it's essential to measure their impact. Use analytics tools to track website traffic, social media engagement, and conversion rates. These metrics can provide insights into what's working and what needs improvement.

Regularly gather feedback from your customers through surveys or direct interactions. Understanding their perception of your brand can help you make necessary adjustments and continue to meet their expectations.

Continuous Improvement

Branding is not a one-time task but an ongoing process. The market and consumer preferences are constantly evolving, so your brand needs to adapt accordingly. Stay updated with industry trends and be open to feedback. Continuously refine your brand strategy to ensure it remains relevant and compelling.

In conclusion, your offer matters significantly, but how you present and support it through effective branding can make all the difference. By implementing these strategies and focusing on building a strong, consistent brand, you can increase your digital offer's visibility and success. Remember, branding is about creating a lasting impression and forming a connection with your audience. With dedication and the right approach, your offer can become an irresistible part of your business strategy.

10

Magnificent Brand Guide

If you don't tell your brand's story clearly and effectively, your potential customers will ignore it as irrelevant or confusing noise, and you will lose business. My strategies focus on how to make an impression that will last—and be profitable.

The key is to ensure that your customer will remember you. Think of "branding" as a story with seven parts. A framework is a way to consistently come up with a useful and impactful message. When used correctly, this framework will change the story customers tell themselves about your business and do more than sell a product or service—it will transform your customer's life and create brand ambassadors who will stick with you for life.

Step 1: Story Matters

Did you know that the human brain uses narratives to understand new information and organize it into meaningful categories quickly and efficiently? When a customer takes the time to learn about your company's history, they are more likely to purchase from you.

What to do: Develop a story that gives a clear path for your customers to engage with and understand your business. Focus on how your product or service will assist your customer in resolving the issues they are experiencing. This will be the most effective way to communicate with your audience.

Step 2: You and Your Company Are Not the Hero

In any story, the character with the most power and authority is not the hero but the guide or mentor. By becoming a trusted advisor to your customer, you can take control of their story, determine what they want or need, and develop a singular, driving focus on your brand.

How to proceed: Assist your customer in navigating the path to self-improvement that your product or service provides. Create a narrative that places them in the spotlight.

Act as their guide to provide the best possible experience for your customers.

Step 3: Types of Problems

Problems can be categorized into three types: external, internal, and philosophical. Customers want to buy solutions that address their problems on all three levels—physical, mental, and emotional.

What to do: Gain an understanding of the frustrations and moral ramifications associated with the external problem your product or service solves. When you engage your customers on a deeper level, they will perceive an increased value from your business.

Step 4: Call to Action

A call to action is necessary to move your customer from passivity. It can be direct or transitional.

What to do: Make the first move by calling the customer to act. Ensure that your call to action is resounding, unambiguous, and unequivocal. If you have the solution, encourage them to make use of it.

Step 5: Planning

Ambiguity, complexity, and even dread can amplify a customer's impression of the risk associated with using your product. Influence the buyer's ultimate choice by reducing these factors.

How to make it appear that you are less dangerous: Design a concise (no more than a few steps) and clear procedure for purchasing and using your product or service. This clarity will help customers feel more confident and less at risk when choosing your offerings.

Step 6: Explaining Success and Failure

People usually make purchases to avoid pain or get closer to pleasure. As a salesperson, you should appeal to your customers' desires by emphasizing what they will lose if they don't buy your product.

What to do: Highlight the negative outcomes if they don't use your product and the positive transformation that will occur if they do. For example, if you're selling a new brand of skincare products, emphasize the potential for better skin health with your product and the problems that might persist without it.

Step 7: Results and Change

Assist customers in realizing that they are on a path to becoming better versions of themselves. Your brand must help them on that journey.

What to do: Show customers how your product or service can solve their problems and help them transform into their ideal selves. Emphasize the transformation and improvement they will experience, building trust and credibility with potential customers.

Step 8: Mission

Without a consistent plot, a "narrative void" can arise. All the brand's efforts should be directed toward the same end.

What to do: Create an in-house brand story that integrates with every facet of your company. Ensure that your team knows where they stand within it. Develop a well-defined purpose statement for your company, and make sure everyone on your team is aware of it. The collective efforts of the brand should be geared toward achieving the same overarching goal.

Step 9: Your One-Liner

A one-liner is a concise statement that encapsulates your brand's mission and value proposition.

What to do: Connect your one-liner to a problem your customer is likely to face. For instance, if you sell products that help people stay healthy, you might connect your one-liner to issues like obesity or heart disease. By doing this, you can show your customer how your company's goals and ideals can help them solve a real-life problem.

Step 10: Your Website

Website engagement is key to keeping customers coming back. The average person's attention span is only eight seconds, so you must make sure your website is engaging and easy to follow.

What to do: Declutter your homepage. Focus on creating a clear and concise message that tells visitors what your business is all about. Make sure your website is easy to navigate so customers can find what they're looking for easily. Add fresh content regularly to show customers that you're active and invested in your business.

Branding Discovery

Understanding the importance of branding discovery is crucial. It helps you create a brand USP (Unique Selling Proposition) and understand how your audience affects brand identity. Market research can influence branding by providing insights into customer preferences and behaviors. Maintaining brand consistency across all channels ensures a cohesive image.

How to proceed: Before beginning branding work, develop a solid branding framework. A branding framework is a set of guidelines that keep your branding efforts focused and on track. It should answer questions like "Who are we trying to reach?" and "What message do we want to send?"

How to Develop a Branding Framework

A robust branding strategy considers every interaction your customers or clients will have with your products or services and lays out a clear plan for how you want them to feel after each touchpoint.

Steps to create a branding framework:

1. Identify who you are as a company and what makes you different from your competition.
2. Understand your target market by identifying their problems and needs.
3. Develop consistent messaging that communicates your
4. uniqueness to your target audience.
5. Ensure your branding efforts are consistent across all channels.

Finding Your Niche

To find your niche, answer these three questions:

1. How does your product or service make your ideal customer's life better?
2. Why should they buy from you instead of your competitor?
3. How can you reach them where they spend their time?

Niche companies that have increased their sales by 5X in the past five years have taken the time to understand how to nail their niche.

Messaging and Consistency

Branding goes beyond a name or logo. It's about your company's global image. This includes the website's design and how customer support answers the phone. A brand must express what a firm stands for and what sets it apart from the competition.

157

Steps to create a strong brand message:

1. Know your values. What differentiates your business?
2. Understand your audience. What do they need? How can you help?
3. Simplify. Your brand message should be brief and
4. straightforward.
5. Ensure consistency. Use your brand message consistently across all media.

Effective Branding Strategies

Creating a brand involves giving the firm and its goods a memorable identity. Brand components include:

- Brand name
- Symbol
- Slogan
- Design palette

Your mission, values, and target audience play a role in picking these elements. Branding encourages client loyalty and can help firms charge more for their products or services because buyers will pay more for superior quality.

Why Brand Products/Services?

Product branding makes your product easily distinguishable from competitors'. It's crucial for businesses that want to establish a strong presence in the marketplace. Branding gives a sense of professionalism and trustworthiness to a product, making it more appealing to potential customers.

The Importance of Storytelling in Branding

A powerful way to enhance your branding strategy is through storytelling. People connect with stories because they are memorable and evoke emotions. When you tell the story of your brand, you give it personality and life. This connection makes your brand more relatable and engaging.

What to do: Share the journey of how your business started, the challenges you faced, and the milestones you achieved. This narrative can create a deeper bond with your audience.

Engaging Your Audience

Engagement is key to maintaining a strong brand presence. Social media platforms are excellent tools for interacting with your audience. Share your stories, respond to comments, and create content that encourages participation. Hosting live sessions, Q&A segments, or behind-the-scenes looks can make your audience feel more connected to your brand.

Measuring Your Branding Efforts

To ensure that your branding efforts are effective, it's essential to measure their impact. Use analytics tools to track website traffic, social media engagement, and conversion rates. These metrics can provide insights into what's working and what needs improvement.

Continuous Improvement

Branding is not a one-time task but an ongoing process. The market and consumer preferences are constantly evolving, so your brand needs to adapt accordingly. Stay updated with industry trends and be open to feedback. Continuously refine your brand strategy to ensure it remains relevant and compelling.

In conclusion, your offer matters significantly, but how you present and support it through effective branding can make all the difference. By implementing these strategies and focusing on building a strong, consistent brand, you can increase your digital offer's visibility and success. Remember, branding is about creating a lasting impression and forming a connection with your audience. With dedication and the right approach, your offer can become an irresistible part of your business strategy.